IMAGES OF WAR

THE BATTLE FOR BURMA 1942-1945

RARE PHOTOGRAPHS FROM WARTIME ARCHIVES

PHILIP JOWETT

Pen & Sword
MILITARY

First published in Great Britain in 2021 by
PEN & SWORD MILITARY
An imprint of Pen & Sword Books Ltd
Yorkshire – Philadelphia

ISBN 978-1-52677-527-6

Typeset by Concept, Huddersfield, West Yorkshire, HD4 5JL.
Printed and bound by CPI Group (UK) Ltd, Croydon, CR0 4YY

Pen & Sword Books Ltd incorporates the Imprints of Aviation, Atlas, Family History, Fiction, Maritime, Military, Discovery, Politics, History, Archaeology, Select, Wharncliffe Local History, Wharncliffe True Crime, Military Classics, Wharncliffe Transport, Leo Cooper, The Praetorian Press, Remember When, White Owl, Seaforth Publishing and Frontline Publishing.

For a complete list of Pen & Sword titles please contact
PEN & SWORD BOOKS LTD
47 Church Street, Barnsley, South Yorkshire, S70 2AS, England
E-mail: enquiries@pen-and-sword.co.uk
Website: www.pen-and-sword.co.uk
or
PEN & SWORD BOOKS
1950 Lawrence Rd, Havertown, PA 19083, USA
E-mail: uspen-and-sword@casematepublishers.com
Website: www.penandswordbooks.com

This book is dedicated to ex-Chindit Private Charles Jowett,
2nd Battalion, The Duke of Wellington's West Yorks Regiment,
who participated in Operation Thursday in 1944.

The front page of a Japanese pictorial magazine shows a crew moving their camouflaged Type 41 75mm regimental gun into position. This gun had been modified from the original 1908 version by putting it onto a more lightweight carriage. It could be broken down into six parts but was light enough to be moved around by its crew from firing position to firing position. (*Author's Collection*)

Contents

Introduction

Japan entered the Second World War in early December 1941 and at the same time brought the USA into the conflict. The Japanese attack on the US Pacific Fleet on 7 December was followed by a highly successful land and sea offensive. This offensive, through South-East Asia and the Pacific, destroyed the imperial control of the Philippines, the Dutch East Indies and British-ruled Malaya, Borneo and Burma. By May 1942 the Japanese ruled an empire that included most of South-East Asia and the islands of the western and central Pacific. British-ruled Burma had never been a priority for the Japanese and the plan was only to take control of the south of the territory for strategic reasons. The unexpected collapse of the British forces in Burma ended in May 1942 with the complete takeover of the whole of the colony. Defeated British and Indian troops, along with some Chinese Nationalist troops sent to aid them by Chiang Kai-shek in early 1942, retreated northwards. They were pursued by the Japanese until their remnants crossed the Indian-Burmese border to try to lick their wounds. Meanwhile the Allies assessed the sheer scale of their defeats and the threat of the new triumphant Japanese Empire.

For the British and their new US allies, the liberation of Burma from Japanese rule was simply not a priority. The Allies' priority was always going to be the defeat of Nazi Germany and Fascist Italy, who were now allied to Imperial Japan. They were far more concerned with the crucial fighting in North Africa in late 1942 and 1943, and Burma simply did not have the strategic value of other fronts during the Second World War. The jungles of Burma were seen as a sideshow and were to be regarded as the 'Cinderella front' for the rest of the war. A main reason for fighting Japan in Burma in 1943 and early 1944 was to try to keep Nationalist China in the war. From the Japanese viewpoint, Burma was seen mainly as a bulwark against Allied attacks into the rest of Japanese-controlled South-East Asia. Increasing speculation about the possibility of invading British India would, of course, involve Burma and the Japanese forces stationed there. It was hoped that Burma's difficult terrain and climate would be sufficient deterrent to any attacks from India.

Burma, some 250,000 square miles in area, was the size of France and Belgium combined and the tropical climate was extreme, with the temperatures in the plains reaching unbearable levels in the summer heat. Rainfall was at least 200 inches per year, increasing to as much as 800 inches in the western region, Arakan. The annual monsoon began in May, with an average rainfall of 20 inches per week, which was usually sufficient to bring any fighting to a standstill. The Burma campaign saw the combatants fighting through the monsoons of 1943, 1944 and 1945. In the western and eastern parts of the country there were great mountain ranges running north to south, covered in thick jungle. The western part of the country on the border of India had mountain ranges that were 600 miles long and 200 miles deep. On the eastern side of Burma, bordering Thailand and China, were high mountains and deep gorges that made travel difficult, to say the least. Several major rivers – notably the Irrawaddy and its tributary the Chindwin, the Sittang and the Salween – ran down the length of Burma. In central Burma there were areas that had little or no jungle, and here rice was grown. The difficult climate in most of Burma, with its heat and high humidity, led to a high incidence of tropical diseases. Malaria, scrub typhus, dysentery and cholera were rife in many areas of Burma, and both Allied and Japanese soldiers suffered terribly during the fighting. As well as these dangers, the presence of blood-sucking and biting and stinging insects and millions of leeches made everyday life even more difficult.

Chapter One

Burma
1942-3

At the end of the disastrous Burma campaign of 1941–2, some 12,000 British and Indian troops and some Chinese marched wearily into the relative safety of India. The vast majority of these troops were in no state to fight, with only 2,000 of them being classed as 100 per cent fit. Most of the others were in various states of exhaustion and were malnourished and disease-ridden. It was not just the military who had suffered during the fighting, and there were thousands of mainly Indian civilians wanting to leave Burma. An estimated 400,000 Burmese and Indians had fled into India, with at least 10,000 dying on the arduous journey. Most of the Indians had been either traders or migrant labourers, and they did not want to stay under the rule of the Japanese. Thankfully for the British military and Indian civilian survivors, once they crossed the Chindwin river the Japanese abandoned their pursuit. The start of the Burmese monsoon also gave the defeated British some breathing space as the Japanese were too weary to fight during the wet season. One Japanese officer, Colonel Hayashi, argued for the continuation of the offensive with the aim of capturing the Indian-Burmese border city of Imphal, to prevent the Allies from using the city as a forward base for ongoing fighting. His arguments found favour with some military planners in Tokyo but the man on the ground, General Iida, knew his men needed a rest. The Japanese offensive came to a virtual stop, but there were clashes between patrols along the Chindwin river. The 23rd Indian Division had moved up to the border from its bases in India to cover the withdrawal of the defeated British-Indian Army, and established a defence line along the Chindwin river behind which the defeated troops began to recover. Many were sent to Imphal, the Indian state capital of Manipur, some 50 miles from the Burmese border, which now took on a new strategic importance as this usually sleepy city became the main base for the Allied war effort on the Burma front and was transformed over a few months into a busy headquarters for the Allied armed forces. The situation in Imphal was chaotic to say the least, with the Japanese expected to move on the town at any time. Fortunately for the British, the Japanese were busy consolidating their position in a territory they had never planned to conquer in the first place. They did not think of pushing into India to 'liberate' the oppressed population of the most prized British imperial possession. Under cover of the 1942 monsoon season, the Allied commanders in Imphal began to improve the infrastructure, which was sorely lacking. Roads leading to the town from the rest of India were improved and three airfields were built to accommodate the first RAF reinforcements that began to arrive.

In addition to building up their forces on the ground in Burma, the Allies also looked to improve the organisation of their high command. General Wavell was replaced as C-in-C India by Sir Claude Auchinleck, and instead took up the role of Viceroy of India. Lord Louis Mountbatten took on the pivotal role of Supreme Allied Commander South-East Asia Command (SEAC). At the same time General Slim was given command of the 14th Army in India, a move that was to prove one of the most positive decisions of the Second World War. General Slim was an inspirational leader, bringing a new, more positive attitude to the Allied forces in India. He was convinced that with good medical care and effective training the condition and morale of his demoralised men would improve. In addition to maximising the troops' performance, Slim also recognised that the infrastructure of the Allied war effort in India had to be greatly developed. Supply dumps had to be built, forward air bases established, existing roads improved and new ones built, and communications updated. The responsibility for operational command decisions on the Burma front was taken away from India Command, leaving its officers free to concentrate on training troops. When Slim took command, he put effective training of the existing and new troops in India at the top of his agenda. Major General Reginald Savory, the former commander of the 23rd Indian Division, was made Inspector of Infantry. In April and May 1943 new roles as 'Inspector of Infantry' and 'Director of Military Training' were filled with competent officers. But even as the British forces in India were making ready to take the war to the Japanese in Burma, other plans were being prepared.

In mid-July 1942 US General Stilwell, who was in charge of Chinese forces in Burma, had conceived a plan to fight the Japanese. His so-called XY Plan was explained to the Allies and to Chiang Kai-shek, the Chinese Nationalist leader. It involved using between twenty and thirty Chinese Nationalist divisions to invade and hold northern Burma. These troops would be retrained by the Allies, supplied with modern weaponry and equipment, and generally well looked after. Stilwell's plan also involved the capture of Rangoon, the Burmese capital, using the Royal Navy (once they had gained control of the Bay of Bengal). On 1 August Chiang Kai-shek reluctantly agreed to Stilwell's plan, although with some reservations. He demanded full British cooperation in the plan, and that the Chinese divisions would be trained and armed by the Allies as promised. Chiang also insisted that his troops must receive good air support from the Allied air forces.

On the other side of the border, in March 1943 the Japanese created a new army-level headquarters, the Burma Area Army, to take control of Japanese forces in Burma. General Masakazu Kawabe was appointed its commander. Under his command were the 15th Army in the north and east of Burma and various units in the south and west of Burma before the formation of the 28th Army in January 1944. Throughout 1943 talks went on in the Japanese headquarters about a possible offensive (or offensives) into India. Arakan in the west of Burma was seen as one route into India, with the main target for any invasion being the important Indian city of Calcutta. Imphal in south-east India was seen as a potential jumping-off point for another advance through the Indian province of Assam.

General Stilwell, the American commander of the Chinese Nationalist Army in Burma in 1942, walks into India. He was accompanied by a hundred people, including his Chinese staff and a number of British, Indian and Burmese military personnel. Included in his party were an American volunteer medic, Dr Seagrave, and nineteen Burmese nurses, who all shared the hardship of the retreat. They arrived in Imphal on 20 May 1942. The ageing commander had lost 14lb during the arduous march. (*US National Archives*)

A British medical officer tries to bring some order to the chaotic situation in an improvised field hospital during the long retreat from Burma to India in 1942. These men are on the veranda of a government building in the town of Pyinmana, which was on the escape route for the Chinese Nationalist troops. Dr Seagrave set up this emergency dressing station, which patched up the soldiers before they struggled on towards the safety of India. (*Author's Collection*)

(**Left**) Dr Ba Maw, the Japanese-installed leader of occupied Burma, stands in his formal dress in front of the pre-1885 peacock symbol of the country. He had been awarded the Order of the Rising Sun with Grand Cordon by the Japanese for his loyalty to them. Ba Maw was a leading pro-independence politician before the war and took the opportunity offered by the Japanese to gain independence for Burma. (*Author's Collection*)

(**Below, left**) Aung San, the young leader of the Thakins (the leading Burmese Nationalists), pictured in the uniform of the Burmese National Army. Along with Ba Maw, he used the Japanese as a vehicle to gain independence for Burma and he served as the commander-in-chief of the BNA. When the war went against the Japanese, he pragmatically made a deal with the Allies and turned the BNA into an anti-Japanese guerrilla force. (*Author's Collection*)

(**Below, right**) The cover of a Japanese pictorial magazine of 1943 features a volunteer of the Burmese Defence Army. Recruited from the Burman population of Burma, the BDA reached a strength of about 10,000 men. When Burma was given its independence by the Japanese, the BDA became the Burmese National Army and was expected to fight alongside the Japanese Imperial Army. (*Author's Collection*)

(**Opposite, above**) In 1943 the Japanese began to recruit volunteers from amongst the population of South-East Asia to bolster their overstretched occupation forces. This group of Wa tribesmen from eastern Burma have been recruited to act as local guards to defend their village against pro-Allied tribal volunteers. They have been issued with captured Chinese rifles but their ammunition was limited in case they turned against the Japanese. (*Author's Collection*)

(**Opposite, below**) A Japanese patrol in 1943. The elephants, driven by local howdahs, were useful for traversing the flooded areas of Lower Burma and were used by both sides during the Burma campaign; at least 4,000 elephants were killed during the war. Later in the war the 14th Army added to their several thousand elephants by adopting those left behind by the retreating Japanese. (*Author's Collection*)

(**Above**) Curious Burmese villagers look on as one of the locals takes a Japanese soldier out into the surrounding countryside. Elephants were commonly used on anti-guerrilla patrols, but in central and southern Burma there was no major guerrilla threat to the Japanese occupation of the country until the end of the war. (*Author's Collection*)

(**Opposite, above**) The lessons of the 1942 campaign in Burma had been hard learned by the British Army and preparations to improve matters were soon put in place. Logistical problems were always going to be an issue in the Far East and the construction of new roads on the India-Burma border was a priority. Thousands of Indian labourers like these were put to work building new roads and improving the existing ones. These roads had to be sturdy enough to handle the military traffic that any campaign to retake Burma would require. (*Author's Collection*)

(**Opposite, below**) Chinese Nationalist troops of X-Force take part in jungle training wearing their newly issued khaki drill uniforms and armed with US-supplied Enfield P-17 rifles and a Thompson sub-machine gun. In general terms the USA supplied the majority of the arms to the Nationalist units in India, while the British supplied uniforms and equipment. The men are wearing the anti-mosquito hoods that were vital in malarial regions of Burma but were not practical to wear in action. (*Author's Collection*)

(**Above**) Chinese Nationalist trainees take part in target practice with their newly issued P-17 rifles at the training base at Ramgarh in India. Recruits began to arrive in India from China in their thousands in July 1942, having been flown across the Himalayas by US transport planes. They joined the 9,000 troops who had retreated into Burma at the end of the 1942 campaign. These men, once they were trained and armed by the Allies, would open up a new front against the Japanese in north-eastern Burma by 1943. (*US National Archives*)

(**Above**) Chinese Nationalist troops undergo training in India in November 1943 in readiness for the planned invasion of northern Burma. Some of these soldiers were survivors of the 1942 campaign, who had retreated with the Allies into India. Others had been flown across the Himalayas – 'over the Hump' – from China to India during 1942 and 1943. They were armed and equipped from Allied sources, with US helmets and weapons and British khaki drill uniforms. (*Author's Collection*)

(**Opposite, above**) General Stilwell inspects soldiers of X-Force, along with the Nationalist General Sun Li-jen, who was one of the few Chinese commanders that Stilwell truly respected. Stilwell had an especially difficult relationship with the Chinese Nationalist leader Chiang Kai-shek, whom he regarded as a 'corrupt' warlord. He did, however, respect the rank and file of the Nationalist Army, whom he saw as 'victims' of their incompetent officers. (*Author's Collection*)

(**Opposite, below**) C-47 Dakotas flew over the Himalayas from India to western China and back again laden with Chinese Nationalist troops and war supplies. During the summer of 1942 only twenty-four C-47s were available to fly 13,000 Chinese troops over the Hump from China to India. The route was extremely dangerous, with planes having to fly at up to 20,000ft to avoid the 15,000ft Himalayan peaks. No fewer than 1,074 planes were lost, along with their crews, when flying over the Hump but their efforts effectively kept China in the war. (*Cody Images*)

Indian recruits are inoculated at a recruiting centre in 1943 before going for basic training and being sent to fight in Europe or closer to home in Burma. The Indian Army expanded from 189,000 in 1939 to 2,500,000 by 1945, with a large number of these serving in Burma between 1942 and 1945. During the 1943–5 campaigns in Burma the 5th, 7th, 17th, 19th, 20th, 25th and 26th Indian Divisions fought as part of the Allied 14th Army. (*Author's Collection*)

A British Army captain instructs new Indian recruits during training in late 1942 as the British and Indian Armies prepared to take the war back to the Japanese in Burma. The defeat of the British and Indian formations in 1942 led to new and innovative training courses that emphasised the need to get troops into the jungle. Many lessons were learned from mistakes made during the earlier campaign and the reasons for the Japanese successes were also studied. It was now important to train the Allied soldiers to take on the Japanese in the very environment in which they excelled: the Burmese jungle. (*Author's Collection*)

Chapter Two

The First Arakan Offensive 1942–3

General Wavell was aware that the 14th Army would not be capable of taking the war to the Japanese in Burma until the dry season of 1943. The survivors of 1942 and newly arrived troops being trained in India would take time to prepare both physically and psychologically. Wavell hoped to wipe away the stigma of defeat in 1942 by taking the offensive and launching a limited advance into Burma. In the event, however, instead of waiting till the next dry season, he ordered an attack in the Arakan border region of western Burma. North-west Arakan, along the Indian border, was the target for the offensive, which was to be undertaken by a single Indian Division, the 14th. Control of the mission was in the hands of Eastern Army Command, which received its instructions from Delhi General Headquarters. General Slim, still settling into his new role, was not allowed to take responsibility for this offensive. Intelligence reports suggested that the 14th Division would face an initial defensive force of just two Japanese battalions; these were the 2nd and 3rd Battalions of the 213th Regiment, whose headquarters lay at the port of Akyab, with a population of 45,000.

On 21 December 1942 the troops of the 14th Division crossed the India-Burma border and began to advance through the marshy, jungle-covered coastal region, their main target the vital port of Akyab. Supporting the advance were a handful of Valentine cruiser tanks of the 146th Regiment of the Royal Armoured Corps. These tanks were designed for desert warfare and were of little use in the jungles of western Burma. At first the army's progress was good as the light Japanese defensive force withdrew towards Akyab. By the 31st they had advanced 150 miles but they were still 60 miles short of Akyab. The Japanese defenders delayed the advance as best they could while waiting for the arrival of reinforcements despatched by their commander, General Iido. By mid-January 1943 Japanese resistance had increased and the 14th Division was beginning to take heavy casualties, especially during their assault on well dug-in Japanese on the Mayu Peninsula, which jutted out into the Bay of Bengal. Allied attacks continued for a month but the losses were becoming unsustainable. By early March the offensive had ground to a halt and the 14th Division was coming under increasing pressure from the Japanese, whose strength was increasing day by day. The 26th Indian Division arrived at the front to reinforce the exhausted units of the 14th, who were for the most part withdrawn back to India. One bright spot for the Allied command was that despite their exhaustion, the 14th Division troops maintained their discipline and withdrew in good order back towards India. There were, however, problems with the hastily organised reinforcements of the 26th Division sent forward to relieve them. Most were poorly prepared and some soldiers reportedly had not even received full basic training.

On 17 March the Japanese in Arakan, made up of a hodge-podge of units of the 55th Division, began a major counter-offensive. This two-pronged attack threatened to envelop the Allied force, which continued to withdraw while fighting a series of rearguard actions. Confused fighting was to continue in the Mayu Peninsula for a further two months as a stalemate developed in Arakan. By early April the Japanese had advanced halfway up the peninsula and had captured the Indian headquarters. After another month of fighting the Allied offensive was finally abandoned and the 26th Division and the remaining elements of the 14th were pushed nearly back to the border. By 17 May all the Allied troops were back at their starting point at Cox's Bazaar, protected by the start of the monsoon season.

The 14th Army's offensive had largely been a disaster, costing 3,000 casualties and the loss of vital equipment. Instead of raising morale, it had reinforced the widely held belief that the Japanese soldier was a superior jungle fighter. Japanese losses were estimated at about 1,500 men. Although the 14th Division had managed to maintain its formation, it was effectively finished as a combat unit. Following a pattern that was to be seen throughout the Burma campaign, its five months of jungle combat had physically and psychologically damaged many of its men. It was to take a while longer for the Allied soldier to realise that the Japanese were not 'supermen' and that they could be defeated, given determination.

(**Opposite, above**) Three river boats, confiscated by the Japanese, at anchor in Akyab harbour in Arakan in early 1943. The harbour at Akyab was an all-weather facility and was highly coveted by both sides in the Burma campaign. There were also a number of well built airfields at Akyab, which gave the town a particularly high strategic value. (Author's Collection)

(**Opposite, below**) The crews of a Hudson Mk III bomber squadron receive their instructions before going on a mission. Hudsons were used in a number of roles by the RAF in Burma but mostly for reconnaissance. A total of fifty-eight had arrived in South-East Asia in late 1941 and the survivors from these were used from 1942 onwards. (Author's Collection)

(**Above**) A large formation of Japanese Ki-21 heavy bombers flies over Burma at the time of the Arakan offensive. In the 1941–2 campaign the Japanese had launched raids on Rangoon using more than sixty Ki-21s. During the summer of 1942 the Japanese Imperial Army Air Force in Burma had two Hikosentais (squadrons) of Ki-21s totalling fifty bombers. (*Cody Images*)

(**Opposite**) A 7,000-ton Japanese freighter in the Bay of Bengal off Rangoon trying to deliver supplies to the Imperial Army was struck by bombs from a US aircraft on 27 February 1943. In this photograph the crew can be seen abandoning the ship. With their relatively small mercantile marine, it was a constant struggle for the Japanese to deliver supplies and armaments to their troops throughout South-East Asia from 1942 to 1945. (*Author's Collection*)

(**Right**) British troops wade across a river during the Arakan fighting in late 1942 or 1943 carrying their Lee Enfield .303 rifles over their heads. The officer has a Webley .303 revolver and his NCO also keeps his Thompson M1928 sub-machine gun clear of the water. These troops faced defeat in the campaign in western Burma but they learnt lessons that would serve them well in the near future. (*Author's Collection*)

Indian troops peer out from the cover of the Burmese jungle during the disastrous fighting in Arakan in the early months of 1943. These men were fighting stripped to the waist in the hot and humid conditions that both sides had to endure in the 1941–5 campaigns. The Indian units in Burma in 1943–5 were a real mix, with some ethnic and religious groups regarded as more warlike than others. Soldiers from Madras state, for example, were more highly regarded than those from the Punjab, and Sikhs were almost universally well regarded by the British. Other nationalities recruited in large numbers included Garhwalis and Rajputs. (*Author's Collection*)

In a posed propaganda photograph in 1943, cheery Lancashire Fusiliers write letters home to their loved ones. Besides facing the still dominant Imperial Japanese Army, they also had to contend with an extremely hostile environment that in the end would kill more of them than did the Japanese. The original caption for the photograph says that the Fusiliers 'fought with distinction, courage and cheerfulness in the difficult jungle warfare of Burma'. (*Author's Collection*)

A Gurkha Bren gunner looks nervously out of his camouflaged foxhole on the Indian-Burmese border in early 1943. He served with the Indian Eastern Army, under the command of Lieutenant General Irwin. The main aim of the Allied offensive into Arakan from December 1942 was to liberate the Mayu Peninsula and Akyab Island. (*Author's Collection*)

A Bren gunner waits for the advancing Japanese during the fighting in the jungle in Arakan in 1943. The webbing sling helped support the 22lb weight of his Bren Mk1 and he was equipped with a large canvas bag to carry his spare magazines. Although the magazine could hold thirty bullets, it was recommended to load one or two less to allow for the gun's smoother running. (*Author's Collection*)

An Indian supply unit crosses a stream in Arakan during the failed offensive by the British 15th Corps. It was sometimes found that new Indian recruits had received little training and they were often commanded by incompetent NCOs. Some officers solved the problem by observing their newly arrived troops for several days and then promoting other ranks who showed initiative or were regarded by their comrades as natural leaders. At the same time they demoted the less able NCOs back into the ranks in an attempt to correct the crude initial selection process. *(Author's Collection)*

In early 1943 RAF Blenheim bombers took part in a raid on the port of Akyab and targeted the Japanese ships in the harbour. At this stage in the Burma campaign the Allies did not yet have the air superiority they were to gain later. The slow and poorly armed Blenheims were easy targets for the Japanese Ki-43 fighters that operated over Burma. (*Janusz Piekalkiewicz Collection*)

Japanese machine-gunners equipped with Taisho Model 11 6.5mm light machine guns on a river boat fire at low-flying RAF aircraft attacking Akyab during the first Arakan campaign. The Model 11 was introduced into service in 1922; it fired 5-round clips, was of limited range and was totally out of date by 1943. (*Cody Images*)

A Japanese machine-gun team fire their Type 92 7.7mm heavy machine gun at Indian troops taking part in the Arakan campaign. Although the Japanese forces in Arakan were strictly limited, they still managed to stop the poorly organised Allied advance. At this stage in the Burma campaign the Japanese still maintained their reputation as superior jungle fighters. (*Cody Images*)

Japanese troops manhandle a 75mm Type 38 howitzer forward during the fighting in Arakan. The almost insufferable conditions faced by both sides challenged even the toughest Japanese and Allied soldiers. Moving heavy weaponry and equipment through the jungles of Burma was one of the greatest tests of the Japanese soldiers' ardour in 1943–5. (*Author's Collection*)

Two Japanese soldiers take cover during a firefight with British troops. One of them has a Lee Enfield .303 rifle. During the Burma campaign the Japanese and their Indian allies in the Indian National Army used large amounts of British weaponry. Some Japanese troops also wore British khaki drill uniforms as theirs wore out in the latter stages of the campaign. (*Author's Collection*)

A Japanese infantry section wades through a swamp during the fighting for the Mayu Peninsula in 1943. They are wearing tropical uniforms with shirt sleeve order and carry all their equipment in their canvas packs. The Japanese defenders were able to outfight the British force sent against them in Arakan. Their performance in the campaign kept the 'jungle supermen' image of the Imperial Army alive for a little longer. (*George Forty*)

Japanese troops move forward at the double carrying heavy kit and with their shoulders and helmets covered in jungle foliage. If they were detected by Allied troops, they would fall to the ground and merge into the undergrowth. Their training emphasised infiltration tactics, which enabled them to get as close as possible to Allied defences before making their final charge. Night attacks were another feature of the Japanese strategy, with their soldiers creeping up on often terrified British and Indian sentries. *(Author's Collection)*

A squad of Japanese troops rushes a jungle clearing to attack an Allied defensive position in Arakan. Attacking a well dug-in position in this way would be costly unless the defenders panicked and fled. Attacks like this were often accompanied by Japanese battle cries, which were of course intended to terrify the waiting defenders. *(Author's Collection)*

A British Army NCO, armed with a Thompson sub-machine gun, moves nervously through the Arakan jungle. His khaki drill uniform looks dry and well pressed, and he wears his side cap jauntily on the side of his head. These factors suggest that he had not been at the front for long before he was photographed by the news cameraman. At just over 10lb, the Thompson was a heavy weapon to carry through the Burmese jungle but it was at least reliable. (*Author's Collection*)

Ground crew of the 50th Air Regiment of the Japanese Imperial Army Air Force are working on a Hayabusa Ki-43 fighter in 1943. In the background Burmese labourers work on the ditches surrounding the unit's runway, probably after an Allied air raid. Like many Ki-43s in service in Burma, this aircraft's paintwork has flaked and the plane looks rather war weary. At this stage in the campaign the Hayabusa was still holding its own against the available Allied planes it faced. (*Author's Collection*)

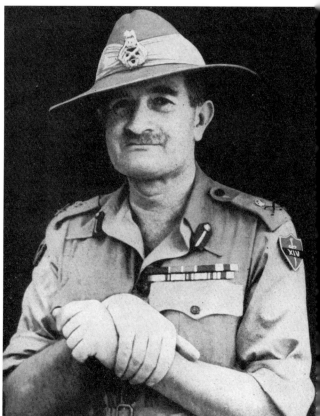

General Sir George J. Giffard, pictured after taking over command of the 11th Army Group from General Irwin. The 11th Army Group commander had responsibility for forces in Burma, Ceylon and the garrisons in the Indian Ocean. Irwin had been sacked largely because of the embarrassing defeat in the Arakan campaign. He had issued a 'no-withdrawal' order to his troops in April as he didn't understand the gravity of the situation there. At the height of the offensive he had asked for obsolete Valentine tanks, thinking they were adequate for service in Arakan. (Author's Collection)

General Sir William Slim, the 52-year-old commander of the 14th Army, sports the badge of his formation on his sleeve in 1943. Slim had joined the Indian Army in 1919 and served as a brigadier in the 1941 fighting in Ethiopia and Syria. In April 1942 he was put in charge of the 15th Indian Corps (part of BURCORPS) and remained in command them until the corps was forced to retreat to Burma. His men took part in the first Arakan offensive in 1943, before Slim was put in charge of the 14th Army in October that year. (Author's Collection)

Chapter Three

Behind Enemy Lines: the Chindits and Burmese Guerrilla Forces 1942–3

During the Allies' recovery period from their defeat in mid-1942, ways were sought to take the war to the Japanese occupation forces. One solution was to harness the pro-British and anti-Japanese feeling amongst some of the minority tribes of Burma. They had suffered at the hands of the Burmese Independence Army that had killed thousands of tribal minority civilians in 1941–2. General Wavell ordered the setting up of an ethnic guerrilla force to operate along the 800-mile long Indian-Burmese border. This force was to be made up of 'friendly' Kachin, Karen and Chin hill tribesmen, many of whom had served in the Burma Frontier Force. Known as 'Victor Force', the 12,000 or so guerrillas were armed and trained by Allied officers. On the north-eastern frontier there were also groups of Naga and Kuki tribesmen who were willing to fight for the British. Scarce arms were issued to the tribal fighters, who soon proved themselves to be a major irritant to the Japanese jungle garrisons. They established jungle bases and fought off attacks on them while also continuing to strike at Japanese bases. They were organised into six Commands, with each commanded by a British staff, which gave them a regular military structure. The Chin Hills where they operated were vitally important as they formed the physical link between Arakan and the Allied base at Imphal. By late 1943, after the failure of the Arakan offensive, the Japanese pressure built against Victor Force. The guerrillas had to withdraw from some of their bases, including those at Falam and Haka, but were bolstered by the arrival of the 1,100-strong Lushai Brigade. This brigade – an exotic mix of regular soldiers of the Indian Army and volunteers from the Chin Levies and Assam Rifles – was under the command of the eccentric Brigadier Marindin, who was described as a 'piratical character'. The tribal fighters were to continue the war in northern Burma until 1944, with their role changing as the war developed.

At the same time another way to hit back at the Japanese in Burma was being developed. It was the brainchild of Major Orde Wingate, who had been an advocate of unconventional military tactics since the 1930s when he helped organise Jewish military forces in Palestine. He had also organised a force of Ethiopian guerrillas in 1940 which helped liberate their country, alongside a Commonwealth Army, in 1941. His idea was to lead regular troops behind Japanese lines to act as guerrillas and to disrupt their logistical network. Wingate named his force the Chindits, a name derived from the Burmese name for the creatures – 'Chinthe' – that stood guard over Buddhist temples. On 8 February 1943 Wingate personally led the 3,000-strong 77th Indian Brigade out of their base at Imphal and over the border into northern Burma. Under the codename Longcloth, the operation was intended to give the Japanese a taste of their own medicine. Officially, the Long Range Penetration Brigade, it was split into Southern and Northern groups. The Southern Group was to distract Japanese garrisons, while the Northern Group attacked the strategic Mandalay-Myitkyina railway. The Chindits were further divided into eight columns, numbered from 1 to 8. They operated individually at times but joined together when necessary. It took a month for both groups to reach the Irrawaddy river, and they then went on to attack the railways, destroying the line at twenty-five points by the end. Large Japanese forces sent to deal with the Chindits began to put heavy pressure on Wingate's force. It was difficult to feed the large numbers of men and obtaining supplies became a major problem. There was a heavy reliance on RAF air drops to keep the Chindits supplied and some of these drops fell into enemy hands. At this stage in the Burma campaign lessons were being learned by the RAF regarding air support operations in what was a relatively new aspect of jungle warfare. Throughout March and into April 'Longcloth' continued, although Wingate had received instructions from Wavell to withdraw from Burma in late March. A 1,000-mile march now followed, with clashes with Japanese units continuing as the Chindits made their long way home to India. The operation was costly; the Chindits suffered 1,000 casualties, and many of the remaining 2,000 men were unfit for further duty. Operation Longcloth was hailed in the British press as a great success, largely to counter the failure of the Arakan offensive. The main success for the Allies, however, lay in unsettling the Japanese Army in Burma. Although they would not admit it, the Chindits had for the first time made the Japanese realise that they were not the only ones capable of jungle fighting.

Happy Kachin volunteers crouch in a village where they have gathered to offer their services to the Allies in 1943. They are armed with their newly issued P-17 rifles as well as the *daal* swords they have brought with them from home. Besides the Kachin, forces were raised from the Karen and their related Karenni populations. Shan and Chin volunteers were also raised but not in the same numbers as the Karen and Karenni, who provided up to 12,000 volunteers. (*Author's Collection*)

A couple of Kachin tribesmen examine their newly issued rifles. The man on the left has a Lee Enfield .303 Mk IV, while his friend has been given an older Mauser-type rifle, perhaps donated by the Chinese. The British found that the minority tribes of Burma were usually more amenable to them than the majority Burman population. (*US National Archives*)

31

Newly recruited Kachin tribesmen bring up supplies. They too have been issued with Lee Enfield rifles and one also has his native 'daal' sword in its scabbard over his shoulder. In the early stage of the employment of guerrilla forces most tribesmen were not issued with uniforms. As the supply situation improved in 1944 and 1945, most guerrilla fighters wore a combination of khaki drill and civilian clothing. (*US National Archives*)

This photograph, taken on 7 July 1943, shows a rescue plane sent to pick up wounded Chindits. The original caption says 'Flying Officer Michael Vlasto talks to Major Scott before taking off with his plane full of sick and wounded.' In the early months of the renewed Burma campaign lessons had to be quickly learned and new techniques developed to keep the Chindits supplied. (*Author's Collection*)

Dakota aircrew prepare to parachute drop supplies to the Chindits. Brigadier Wingate demanded that the crews should drop the supplies, like Father Christmas, 'down the chimney'. If the supplies dropped even a short distance from the landing zones which had been cleared in the jungle, they might be impossible to retrieve or fall into Japanese hands. *(Cody Images)*

Men of a Chindit unit rest by a river during Operation Longcloth and take the opportunity to wash their uniforms and bathe themselves. In the foreground of the photograph is the RAF signal section that was attached to No. 3 Column and sent messages back to its HQ. The eight columns that made up the Chindit force were a mixture of British, Indians and Gurkhas. *(Author's Collection)*

Brigadier Orde Wingate, wearing his distinctive cork sun helmet, holds an informal conference with some of his officers on the India-Burma border in the build-up to Operation Longcloth in 1943. Wingate was one of those unconventional officers who emerge in conflicts and question the standard way of making war. He was fortunate to have an enthusiastic sponsor in the form of Winston Churchill, who recognised the brilliance of this enigmatic commander. (*Author's Collection*)

Japanese troops trudge up a hill in the Shupii mountain range while on operations against the first Chindit operation of 1943. The Japanese responded with force against the Chindits and sent large numbers of troops into the jungle against them. Japanese commanders were indignant at the arrogance of the British in sending their soldiers behind their lines. These soldiers are carrying heavy kit through an area which has recently been cleared of trees, making progress much easier. (*George Forty*)

(**Above, left**) A Japanese forward observer telephones his regimental headquarters from his trench during the operation to try to counter the Chindits. The first Chindit operation was countered by the Imperial Army's 18th Division, whose troops had captured Singapore in 1942. It came as a serious shock to the Japanese commanders that the British soldiers they despised were now capable of operating successfully behind their lines. (*Author's Collection*)

(**Above, right**) A warrant officer of the 77th Indian Brigade jokes with one of his men after having been flown out of the Burmese jungle at the end of Longcloth. The sheer relief of returning from such a gruelling operation is clear to see in the faces of both soldiers. After the end of Operation Longcloth many of the Chindits were found to be unfit for future front-line service. Wingate stated that three months of service in the jungles of Burma was often enough to render a soldier incapable of further front-line service. (*Cody Images*)

(**Opposite**) A column of Gurkhas moves through the hills of central Burma during Operation Longcloth. The 3/2nd Gurkhas and a company of Gurkha muleteers were included in Major Calvert's No. 3 Column of the Chindit force. When the Gurkhas retreated back towards India, they suffered a large number of casualties as the pursuing Japanese troops attacked them. There were 446 losses, although 150 of these eventually filtered back through the jungle to safety, while another forty-five escaped after capture. Seventy Gurkhas were taken prisoner by the Japanese. Their fate was not recorded, although their captors were known for their harsh treatment of prisoners. (*Cody Images*)

(**Above**) Two Chindits march through the jungle with their trusty mules on 1 March 1943 during Operation Longcloth. A large number of mules came from India but the Chindits preferred those bought from neutral Argentina and the USA. During Longcloth the mules were reported to have given away Chindit positions with their braying. Before the 1944 operation most mules had their voiceboxes surgically removed by the Indian Army Veterinary Department to solve the issue. (*Cody Images*)

(**Opposite, above**) Brigadier Mike Calvert and two of his officers of No. 3 Column pause to survey the devastation wrought by their Chindits in a Japanese-held village. Calvert had met his mentor Orde Wingate in February 1942 in Burma, where he was running a commando school. After the retreat from Burma, Wingate appointed Calvert as his second-in-command, realising that his commando experience was invaluable to the Chindits. (*Cody Images*)

(**Opposite, below**) An exhausted-looking Chindit, with bayonet fixed on his Lee Enfield rifle, moves at speed past a Buddhist shrine. Chindits, according to their commander, had to be 'Strong enough to inflict a damaging blow, sufficiently small and mobile enough to hide and evade enemy reactions.' The Chindits had begun their first operation largely believing that Japanese soldiers were superior to them in jungle warfare. By the end of the operation they had learned that the jungle was just as difficult an environment for the Japanese as it was for them. (*Cody Images*)

(**Opposite, above**) According to the original caption, this column of Chindits burned their boats before crossing the river, with their mules carrying most of their supplies. They are travelling light, with only their small arms and light machine guns, so they can move as swiftly as possible. Included in their armoury are sticks of dynamite, which they used to blow up bridges and Japanese arms dumps. (*Cody Images*)

(**Opposite, below**) Mixed Chindits and Kachin guerrillas are flown back to the safety of India after a few weeks in the Burmese jungle. Although Operation Longcloth had been a disappointment in many ways, the Japanese had learnt a grudging admiration for these men. At the end of the campaign the Chindits were worn out and needed a long period of rest and recuperation. (*Cody Images*)

(**Above**) Chindits smile for the camera, their sheer relief at having survived their mission evident to all. The terrible jungle conditions they endured in 1943 and 1944 left them vulnerable to a myriad of diseases, with most suffering a combination of illnesses simultaneously. Amoebic dysentery was a horrible, debilitating condition that weakened the sufferer as well as making good hygiene impossible. One platoon even cut out the seats of their trousers because of the severe dysentery they suffered during the fighting. (*Cody Images*)

Chapter Four

The Air War
1943–5

During the 1941–2 campaign in Burma the Japanese Army and Navy Air Forces had swept from the skies the Royal Air Force's older fighters and bombers, which simply could not compete with the newer types of Japanese aircraft. The main Japanese fighter, the Ki-43, could even outperform the Hurricanes that made up the RAF's main fighter force before November 1943. In that month the first Spitfire fighters arrived in Burma and the situation changed. Over the next three months they destroyed a hundred Japanese planes while losing only five pilots.

At the end of 1943 the Japanese still had 370 planes in Burma but their numbers were beginning to decline. Ki-43s were still the main type in service with the Japanese, and they were to soldier on alongside newer types until 1945. Most new types of Japanese fighter were increasingly sent to the Pacific as Burma had a much lower priority. The other dominant Japanese fighter in 1941–2 was the Zero, which was flown mainly by the Navy Air Force. Few of these were seen over Burma, but they were being outclassed in other theatres anyway. Their weaknesses were revealed by the US pilots of the Flying Tigers Squadron over Burma in 1942. Many of these pilots passed on the knowledge they had picked up in action, and the Zero saw little service. In 1943 a few were seen over Burma escorting bombers and some took part in several strafing missions in May 1944.

Japanese pilots were admired by their public as the 'Samurai of the Sky' and most followed the traditional Bushido Code. This old-fashioned attitude worked against the Japanese air crews in several ways. One result of it was the pilots' dislike of using cloud cover during attacks as it was regarded as dishonourable. Many pilots did not check that their machines were serviceable before taking off, regarding such checks as beneath them, and the province of the ground crews. However, the often-quoted belief that Japanese pilots refused to wear parachutes was a myth. Parachutes were issued and the official line was that they should be worn, although it was not strictly imposed. The pilots' rationale for not wearing them was more a matter of practicality than part of some suicidal Samurai code. Some pilots found the parachutes constricting and said that without them they felt part of their aircraft. Others cited the fact that even if they were to parachute from their stricken planes, there was little if any chance of rescue. There was no such thing as air sea rescue in the Japanese air forces and a pilot who landed in the sea was on his own.

By 1944 the Japanese 4th Air Brigade in Burma was made up of four air regiments: the 50th with Ki-43 fighters, the 10th with Ki-45 ground attack planes, the 8th with Ki-48 medium bombers and the 14th with Ki-21 medium bombers. The 7th Air Brigade also comprised four air regiments: the 81st with Ki-46 reconnaissance planes, the 31st and 21st with Ki-43 fighters and the 64th with Ki-44 fighters. There were also two regiments with Ki-21 medium bombers. In October 1944 the Japanese were still receiving limited air reinforcements but their strength was reducing by 10 per cent every month. By November 1944 the Japanese had only 125 planes, their number further reduced by April 1945. As the last phase of the fighting in Burma began, there were only fifty Japanese aircraft still operating there.

On the Allied side the situation in 1942 was dire, with few RAF airfields in usable condition. The first priority was to repair damaged air bases in India and to build new ones, with 150 being constructed by the end of the year. During the 1942–3 Arakan campaign the RAF was still using outdated planes, with eight squadrons of Hurricane fighters and two of Blenheim light bombers. Blenheim bombers were described as 'museum pieces' and had been obsolete since 1940. Regardless of this, they had to struggle on until newer aircraft could be delivered to Burma. Until the arrival of the Spitfires the RAF had to make do with Hurricanes and Kittyhawk III fighters, with a few Spitfires that had to be used for reconnaissance only. Spitfire Mk V fighters arrived in Burma in the autumn of 1943 and were followed in the new year by Mk VIIIs.

In November 1943 there was only a single RAF transport squadron available to supply the whole of the 14th Army. In addition, there were two USAAF troop carrier squadrons that were available to support the Chinese Army in India, known as X-Force. Transport planes were the most important air element in the Burma campaign and the shortage of them was a constant problem. Louis Mountbatten tried to beg, borrow or steal C-47 Dakotas from anywhere that he could. Crucially, he managed to get on loan seventy-nine C-47s from the Mediterranean theatre, plus another fifty-nine diverted from their duties transporting men and supplies over the Hump. The transports were available through the US Air Transport Command, which received a windfall when seventy C-47s were found lying idle on airfields in Trans-Jordan. These planes were snapped up before they could be claimed by the planners organising Operation Overlord. Mountbatten asked in May 1944 to be allowed to retain the transports from the Mediterranean, or twenty planes along with the fifty-nine taken from the Hump airlift.

At the beginning of 1944 the RAF and Indian Air Force had four squadrons (the 1st, 28th, 34th and 42nd) of Hurricanes at Imphal and Palel, plus two squadrons of Spitfires (the 81st and 136th) and one of Beaufighters (the 176th) at Kangala and Sapam. During 1944 the RAF received welcome support from the USAF No. 1 Commando Group, which was made up of a hundred light aircraft, thirty Mustang P-51 fighters, twenty Mitchell B-25 medium bombers and thirty transports including twenty C-47 Dakotas. There were also six Sikorsky helicopters – a new type of aircraft that was usually used to evacuate casualties. In addition, 150 gliders were delivered to the commando group in preparation for the large-scale landing of troops behind enemy lines. The commando group was formed to support General Stilwell's Chinese expeditionary forces fighting in northern Burma from 1943 to 1945. By December 1944 the main Allied air support was provided by the thirty-seven squadrons of 221 Group RAF. There were five squadrons of B-24 medium bombers, two squadrons of Thunderbolt fighters and two squadrons of Mustang fighters operating from Arakan. There were also fourteen squadrons of ground support planes, including two squadrons of Beaufighters, two of Mosquitos and two of Thunderbolts. Operating from Khumhirgram and Wangjing were four squadrons of Thunderbolts and four squadrons of medium bombers.

As the fighting in Burma went on, the Allied pilots began to gain enough experience to take on their 'superior' Japanese counterparts. By August 1943 pilots had also learned the skills that were necessary to fly over the jungle and to fly in the severe weather conditions of the monsoon season. In addition, they began to receive material assistance due to the Allies' superior technology. They had the advantage of an efficient meteorological service which could provide them with accurate weather forecasts up to 1,000 miles away. By 1945 Allied aircraft losses resulted mainly from accidents and crashes, not enemy aircraft. Many planes crashed due to the adverse weather conditions encountered in the Burma theatre. For example, one Beaufighter squadron which had a particularly high attrition rate lost seventy-five air crew over an eighteen-month period.

(**Above**) Armourers load 20mm ammunition into the wings of a Hurricane that may have been converted into the fighter-bomber role. As the Hurricane was replaced in service with the RAF in North Africa and on home service in late 1942 some were available to send to the Far East. Although they retained their wing cannon, they were converted to carry bombs under their wings and renamed Hurribombers. (*Author's Collection*)

(**Opposite, above**) A Hurribomber is serviced at a Indian airfield in early 1943. Given the designation IIC, Hurribombers were fitted with long-range fuel tanks and had a conventional 250lb bomb under each wing. They could also drop napalm bombs. These sturdy aircraft with their 20mm cannon had already given great service in North Africa and were a potent weapon in the air war over Burma. A new version known as the Mk IID was introduced in March 1943 with strengthened wings that could accommodate 40mm cannon. (*Author's Collection*)

(**Opposite, below**) This RAF Mohawk Mk IV fighter belonged to either the 5th or the 155th Squadron and is seen here in its last months of front-line service in the summer of 1943. The Mohawk was the RAF version of the Curtiss P-36, which was first delivered to the USAF in 1938. Mohawks were obsolete by the time they were phased out in December 1943 but had given good service to the RAF when little else was available. (*Author's Collection*)

Newly arrived Supermarine Spitfires fly along the Burmese coast, armed with two 20mm cannon and four .303 machine guns. In the autumn of 1943 some Mk Vs arrived in Burma and these were followed in January 1944 by the improved Mk VIIIs. The performance of the newer Spitfires made what was already a fine fighter into a much improved aircraft. For instance, the original Mk I took 15 minutes to climb to 25,000ft whereas the Mk VIII took only 7 minutes. (*Author's Collection*)

The Japanese Imperial Air Force fighter ace Satoru Anabuki – 'Flower of the Youth Flyers' – pictured in front of his aircraft at the height of his fame. His claim of fifty-two kills over Burma and India has been disputed recently but he certainly was one of the best Japanese pilots. Aircraft shot down by Satoru during his time in Burma were: eleven P-40s, twenty-five Hurricanes, four Blenheim bombers, one Wellington bomber, four B-24 bombers and one B-25 bomber. Other fighters he claimed to have destroyed were three P-36s, one Spitfire and one P-38 Lightning. (Author's Collection)

Mitsubishi Ki-21 medium bombers fly over Burma in 1943. At this stage of the war the Japanese could still counter the improving Allied air effort. The Ki-21 had given good service in the 1941–2 campaign in Burma but a year later it was outclassed by Allied aircraft. It had a top speed of only 297mph and as the war progressed it was deployed whenever possible in areas where enemy fighters would not be encountered. (Author's Collection)

(**Opposite, above**) A Kawasaki Ki-48 light bomber of the 8th Air Brigade flies over southern Burma in 1944. By now the Japanese were rapidly losing control of the air war. Codenamed 'Lily', the Ki-48 served in a number of roles during the war, notably as the dive-bomber version called the Ki-48-II. Although this plane was outmatched by 1944, it continued to be produced until October that year. (*Author's Collection*)

(**Opposite, below**) A Ki-48 bomber is prepared to go on a sortie in 1944. It was part of a diminishing Japanese Army bomber force. By the last year in the war aircraft like this were being shot out of the sky in increasing numbers, and leaving a plane out in the open like this was asking for trouble from the large number of Allied ground attack planes operating over Burma in 1944. (*Cody Images*)

(**Above, left**) Smiling Japanese ground crew load their squadron's Ki-48 light bomber. The Ki-48 had a total bomb load of 661lb. By late 1944 the Ki-48 was restricted to the 8th Hikosentai and most bombing raids were confined to three or four planes. It was difficult for larger numbers to get to their targets when the air above Burma was totally dominated by Allied aircraft. (*Author's Collection*)

(**Above, right**) Fellow pilots shake hands with the pilot of a Ki-48 light bomber while his observer raises his fist in defiance, even as the air war was turning against the Japanese in 1944. The morale of most Imperial Army personnel remained high until the end of the war in Burma. Most pilots continued to fly combat missions until they were killed in action or fell ill from tropical diseases. Their Allied opponents at least got rest periods as their personnel were rotated to give them a chance to recover their strength and nerves. (*Author's Collection*)

A Consolidated Liberator B-24 bomber is loaded with bombs ready for a raid on the Burmese capital, Rangoon. The RAF flew Type III versions of the US-manufactured bomber, while the USAF flew the D type. With a bomb load of up to 8,000lb, the Liberator was to prove a devastating weapon against the largely undefended Japanese positions. *(Author's Collection)*

Flight Lieutenant A. Torrance of 'A' Flight, 27th Squadron, climbs aboard his Mosquito FB-VI attack bomber in March 1944. He is dressed rather unconventionally in cotton overalls and a slouch hat, and has a Webley revolver slung over his shoulder to defend himself in the event of a crash behind enemy lines. His unit was stationed at Parashuram in India, from where they flew missions over northern Burma, attacking any Japanese positions using their deadly 20mm cannon. (*Author's Collection*)

Ground crew cover the fuselages of their Hurricane fighters during the first Arakan campaign in late 1942/early 1943. During the 1941–2 campaign the Hurricane was the backbone of the RAF's fighter force. From 1943 the majority of the Hurricanes that remained in Burma were converted to the ground attack role. In this new role they served the RAF well until more modern aircraft could be put into service during the last two years of the campaign. (Author's Collection)

Chapter Five

Operation Thursday:
the Second Chindit Operation
1944

Following the mixed results of Operation Longcloth, the jury was out on the merits of another long-range penetration operation. Wingate, who had been promoted to the rank of major general, began lobbying strongly for permission to launch a second operation but ran into strong opposition from both General Slim and Lord Mountbatten. Slim thought that a second Chindit operation would not aid his plan to defeat the Japanese in northern Burma, and that the scarce aircraft and men needed for a large-scale operation would be better used elsewhere. Heated discussions took place among the three men between December 1943 and February 1944. Slim and Wingate also met on a number of occasions and argued the viability of and need for another Chindit operation. Wingate's influence with Winston Churchill meant that he could argue from a position of strength against those who objected to his plan. The problem was how best to employ the Chindits to assist the Allied war effort and in the end a plan was formulated. Known as Operation Thursday, it would see gliders landing troops to disrupt the Japanese war effort in northern Burma. Whereas Longcloth had deployed 3,000 men, Thursday would involve about 23,000 men in six brigades. The operation's main objectives were threefold: to support General Stilwell's Chinese troops' attack on the strategic town of Myitkyina; to assist the crossing of the Salween river by the Chinese Y-Force from Yunnan province into eastern Burma; and to destroy the supply lines and communications of the Japanese in northern Burma. Five of the six brigades were to be flown into landing areas in northern Burma where bases and airfields would be established. The other brigade had already set off from its base in India to march 450 miles to support the airborne landing brigades. Air support for Thursday came from the US 1st Air Commando, which had been established to support all operations in northern Burma. Three main landing sites had been chosen that were inaccessible to any Japanese troops and aircraft. They had all been identified by aerial reconnaissance as suitable for adaptation as airfields. In preparation for the coming operation, Japanese airfields within range of the landing sites were bombed. Once established, the landing sites would be complemented by the setting-up of well fortified strongholds to hold off any Japanese attacks. All the landing sites were named after major roads throughout the free world. The codenames of the projected bases in Burma were Piccadilly, Broadway, Chowringhee and Templecombe. The 77th Indian Brigade was to split into two and be flown in gliders to establish Piccadilly and Broadway, which were situated to the north-east of Indaw. The 111th Brigade was to be flown into another base, Chowringhee, which was to the west of Indaw. The 16th Brigade, which had been on the move since February, would establish their own base, Aberdeen, north-west of Indaw. Unfortunately aerial reconnaissance showed that the projected landing field for Piccadilly was covered in heavy teak logs so it could not be used. (This site had been used during the 1943 operation and the Japanese had most likely blocked it to stop its possible reuse.) The brigade destined for Piccadilly was at the last minute diverted to land at Broadway instead. Once established, the Chindits would set out in 400-man columns to attack Japanese strategic targets.

The operation began on 5 March when the 77th Indian Brigade and part of the 111th Long Range Penetration Brigade landed by glider at Broadway. Over the next six nights a total of 9,500 men and 1,100 mules were flown in 600 C-47 sorties by 83 aircraft and 100 gliders. Losses were light, with a casualty rate of only 1 per cent in what was a highly dangerous operation. The plan was to fly the 3rd West African Brigade to Aberdeen as a single unit to reinforce the Chindits, but instead on 11 March one battalion was sent to each of the three brigades already in place. It was a week before the first Japanese units began attacking the Chindit bases but soon they were all under attack. In total, there were twelve Japanese battalions in the anti-Chindit force, with more on the way. On the 12th they attacked Broadway and the following day they began to assault Chowringhee. Heavy fighting continued through-out March, with the Chindits abandoning some bases and establishing other strong-holds, named White City and Blackpool. On 24 March a second wave of 6,000 troops, 850 animals and 550,000lb of supplies were landed. Fighting continued through April, May and June, with the Chinese advance on the town of Myitkyina being aided by Chindit attacks on the Japanese rear. The Chindits also moved against the town of Mogaung to the west of Myitkyina, which they captured in late May. By late June the Chindits were exhausted and a phased withdrawal began. By late August they were all back in India and those who were fit were sent to reinforce 14th Army units.

Although Operation Thursday was regarded by many in Burma as a let-down, the reality was a mixed result. Some said it achieved little apart from aiding the capture of Myitkyina (see Chapter 6), but the Japanese complimented General Wingate on his timing of the operation. They said that if it had been launched a week or so earlier, the attack on Imphal (see Chapters 7 and 8) would have been delayed, and a week or so later then the Japanese moving northwards to Imphal would have been able to move more supplies up to the front line, thereby swinging the fighting in their favour.

Although the operation was not a wholesale success, this was no reflection on the brave Chindits. They suffered the usual high level of casualties, with 1,000 killed and 2,400 wounded, and a further 450 missing. Many of the returning Chindits had malaria, dysentery and jungle sores, with some men having all three!

A C-47 Dakota transport plane drops supplies by parachute for the Chindits during their second operation. Air-drops like this kept the Chindits in the field. The people in charge of this relatively new way of supplying troops in the field had to streamline their methods as they went along, and Allied air superiority from 1943 onwards certainly helped. (*Cody Images*)

(**Above**) Once the Chindits had been flown into the jungle, they began to build the air-strips that were to be their lifeline during Operation Thursday. These men belonged to the 5318th Provisional Unit, which was tasked with building air-strips. Hacking out from the jungle a suitable landing ground for C-47 transports and other supply planes was one of the first priorities for the Allied troops. The transports would then bring supplies in and take the wounded and sick out to field hospitals. It was important to keep the casualty rate as low as possible after the high attrition rate during the 1943 operation. (*Cody Images*)

(**Opposite, above**) A Chindit carries his Gurkha comrade to a waiting Sentinel light plane, a type that was widely used for casualty evacuation during Longcloth. The evacuation of wounded soldiers by air saved thousands of lives during the Burma campaign. Sentinels (or Stinson L-5s as they were more widely known) were US planes that were supplied to the RAF in large numbers. They performed spotting, communications and ambulance duties during the Burma campaign. (*Author's Collection*)

(**Opposite, below**) Some of the US pilots who flew the gliders during Operation Thursday pictured resting in front of one of their crashed CG-4 gliders at the Broadway landing site. They were armed in order to defend themselves if they were forced to land their gliders behind Japanese lines. The gliders were towed behind C-47 transports. Earlier attempts to tow two at a time were abandoned after a number of crashes. (*Cody Images*)

Two Japanese soldiers of the 18th Division fire their 50mm Type 89 mortar in the direction of a Chindit patrol. Mortars were a useful weapon in the jungles of Burma, the Type 89 particularly so as it weighed only 10lb. Its nickname was the 'knee mortar' as it was reported to be capable of being fired from the knee or thigh, though if anyone was foolish enough to do so, the recoil would break his leg or shatter his knee. (*US National Archives*)

The crew of an anti-aircraft version of the US Browning .5in heavy machine gun pictured at a temporary headquarters during Operation Thursday. This water-cooled version of the standard machine gun was fitted with anti-aircraft sights, and in this case a small shield. Equipment like this was flown into the zone of operations in gliders, which also brought in the majority of the infantry. In the distance is a jungle hut of the type that would serve as officers' quarters or as a field hospital during the operation. (*Author's Collection*)

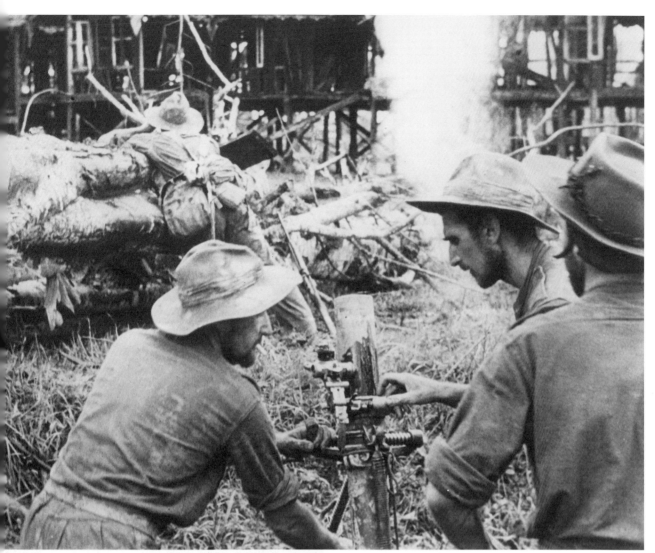

The crew of a 3in mortar give their comrades support from a village that had been turned into a Chindit stronghold. Mortars were a vital support weapon in the close jungle fighting in Burma. This medium mortar could be broken down into three parts – the base, firing tube and stand – which allowed it to be carried for short distances. (*Cody Images*)

A Japanese telegraph operator of the 18th Army at work in a jungle base. He is using a Type 95 set, which was in service with smaller units and used a telephone to listen to incoming messages. It was the 18th Army that was mainly responsible for countering the Chindit operations in 1943 and 1944. The army had fought in South-East Asia from December 1941 and its troops were weary of fighting. (*Author's Collection*)

(**Above**) Chindits carry a comrade in a stretcher. Many wounded men were airlifted away from the front line and back to first aid stations. The strain of the fighting shows on their faces but they also demonstrate the determination needed to operate in the jungles of Burma. Living in the jungle and attacking the Japanese at night, they employed all the skills they had learnt from their experienced officers. (*Cody Images*)

(**Opposite, above**) Three Chindit officers hold a pre-operation meeting in the aftermath of the death of their leader, Major Orde Wingate, who had been killed in a plane crash on 24 March. On the left is Colonel Phil Cochran, who took command of the Chindits after Wingate's death, while in the centre, holding the map, is Captain John Birkitt. Cochran was known as the 'Wing' of the 'Wing and Beard Team', which saw a close partnership between him and the enigmatic Wingate. (*Author's Collection*)

(**Opposite, below**) According to the original caption for this photograph, it shows British, West African and Gurkha troops arriving to be loaded onto C-47s and transported to the Broadway Chindit base. Broadway became the most important base for the 1944 operations and came under heavy attack from the Japanese. This led to the temporary end of flights in and out of the base until the Japanese could be pushed far enough away from Broadway's defensive perimeter. (*Cody Images*)

Concerned Chindits look after their wounded and exhausted comrade, waiting for air evacuation. He had been carried on an improvised stretcher from the front line to one of the main bases supporting the mobile columns during Operation Thursday. When the evacuation planes landed, they were often under fire from unseen Japanese in the surrounding jungle. Sometimes hand-to-hand fighting went on only a few hundred feet from the landing strips. (*Cody Images*)

Chinese troops are evacuated from the front line, along with their wounded comrades, by C-47 transports. The wounded were taken to field hospitals in India, while their fit comrades were rested in case they were needed again at the front. Nationalist troops of X-Force were in the main found to perform well, having received good training in India from 1942. Mountbatten had argued constantly for more transport planes to keep the Chindits, Merrill's Marauders and Chinese troops supplied. (*Author's Collection*)

An exhausted Chindit waits to be flown out of one of the bases established during Operation Thursday. Although they were better supplied during the second Chindit operation than during Operation Longcloth, the jungle still took its toll. From their main bases at Broadway, Aberdeen and Chowringhee, Chindit columns had dispersed in various directions to disrupt the Japanese fighting against the Chinese Nationalist and US forces in northern Burma. (*Cody Images*)

Chindits queue patiently to be evacuated from one of Operation Thursday's air bases at the end of the campaign. Although the efficient supply operation meant that the Chindits were better looked after than during the 1943 operation, they were still exhausted. Wingate had estimated that the maximum time that soldiers could expect to survive in jungle conditions was twelve weeks. (*Cody Images*)

A C-47 Dakota transport plane, carrying Chindits back to India, flies above a Burmese river. A shortage of transport planes on all fronts during the Second World War meant that they were often fought over by the various Allied armies. During Operation Thursday a total of eighty-three C-47s flew repeated missions to the landing zones and back. Burma was given a low priority and the commanders had to argue constantly to have more aircraft sent to the Far East. (*Cody Images*)

Chapter Six

Northern Burma 1943–4

General Stilwell, the chief of staff of the Chinese Army and military adviser to the Chinese leader Chiang Kai-shek, had withdrawn into India in May 1942. He was joined by those Chinese troops he had commanded during the 1942 fighting in Burma who were not able to return to China. Stilwell, his pride hurt by having to retreat from the Japanese and determined to take the war back to them, was now given a new responsibility by President Roosevelt: to organise the Chinese-Burma-India (CBI) theatre of war. Knowing that he could not hope to organise Chinese involvement in Burma from China, Stilwell decided instead to bring Chinese troops to India, where they could be trained to fight in Burma. One of Chiang Kai-shek's principal motives for fighting in Burma was to re-establish the opening of the Burma Road. The main route for Allied arms supplies to Nationalist China, this road had been closed by the Japanese. Stilwell wasted no time in assembling all the Chinese troops he could muster at an Indian training base at Ramgarh. In February 1943 Chiang Kai-shek agreed to send Nationalist troops to fight in Burma in exchange for military 'Lend Lease' aid. By early April Stilwell had formulated a plan, which he presented to Chiang Kai-shek in China. His suggestion was that 100,000 Chinese troops be flown to India, then trained, equipped and armed by the Allies. With good food and living conditions, and positive instruction by US personnel, helped by the issue of new uniforms, equipment and modern US weapons, the Chinese soldiers' morale was raised to a new level. The recruits were formed into a new formation known as X-Force, which would be joined by a small US contingent based on the Chindits.

The perceived success of the first Chindit operation in 1943 had reached US President Roosevelt's attention. It was decided to create a US force in the image of the Chindits and the 5307th Composite Unit, or 'Galahad Force', was quickly raised. The unit was nicknamed 'Merrill's Marauders' after its commander, Colonel Merrill. It was raised from diverse US Army personnel who had been serving in the south-west Pacific and Trinidad. The 'volunteers' were trained in India by British instructors who had helped to train the Chindits. During training some Marauders misbehaved themselves, gaining a reputation for ill-discipline, with 10 per cent of the strength deserting.

By the time they were ready to go into action there were 3,000 volunteers in three battalions, each divided into two columns. They were given 700 mules, although none of the Marauders had any experience in dealing with the difficult animals.

In September 1943 the newly retrained and equipped Chinese 22nd and 38th Divisions were transferred from Ramgarh to Ledo in south-east India. Both divisions had served in Burma in 1942 and their troops were regarded as the best available in China. From Ledo the two divisions crossed into north-eastern Burma and on into the Upper Hukawng Valley. The 38th Division made contact with units of the Japanese 18th Division in the Hukawng Valley in December. At the same time Stilwell arrived at the front line to take personal control of the fighting. The 22nd and 38th Divisions continued their advance down the valley, along with Merrill's Marauders. To the south of the Hukawng Valley were the two objectives of the Chinese-US offensive: Mogaung and Myitkyina. Myitkyina and its airfield were especially important to Stilwell's plans as control of the town was the key to air power in northern Burma. To support Stilwell's offensive, the Second Chindit operation (Thursday) was launched to distract the 18th Division facing the Chinese. During January 1944 Stilwell's troops maintained a steady advance down the Hukawng Valley and were halfway down it by February. They had taken the town of Taro 100 miles to the north-west of Myitkyina, and Merrill's Marauders had assembled in the north to form a flanking force to support the Chinese advance. Early March saw the Chinese 22nd and 38th Divisions capture the town of Maingkwan at the southern end of the Hukawng Valley. On their left flank Merrill's Marauders crossed the Tanai river and took the town of Walabaum, only 60 miles from Myitkyina. Fighting for this town was ferocious, with Japanese bayonet charges and hand-to-hand fighting. Both sides were short of food, with inadequate supply lines on both sides coming under strain. On 6 May the town of Ritpong, only 30 miles from Myitkyina, fell. As the offensive continued against heavy Japanese resistance, the US-Chinese force was supported by a unit of Chindits coming up from the south. On 17 May the newly arrived Chinese 50th Division, along with units of Merrill's Marauders, captured Myitkyina airfield, but the town itself and its 700-strong Japanese garrison continued to resist. Over the next few weeks the Japanese were able to build up their garrison to a strength of 4,000 men. Stilwell now ordered that the Marauders were to take part in frontal assaults against the Japanese defences. This was deeply resented by the men, who did not think their lives should be wasted in costly attacks against well dug-in defenders. Both sides now settled down into a siege, which was to last for eleven weeks. On 26 June Mogaung to the west of Myitkyina fell to a mixed force of Chindits and the 38th Division, and the 38th then moved eastwards to help finish off the defenders at Myitkyina, 30 miles away. It took another five weeks to take the town. Finally the Japanese withdrew, their forces having been reduced to 300 fit fighters. It had been a costly victory for the besieging force as well, with the Chinese losing 4,000 killed or wounded. The

Marauders lost 1,200 killed, wounded or sick, and were basically finished as a fighting force. On the Allied side there was also a high level of sickness, the Americans suffering 1,000 while the Chinese had only 200. The higher proportion of US sick to Chinese was down to the fact that the former didn't habitually boil their water. Chinese troops, regardless of the battle conditions, always boiled their water and also cooked their food, while the US troops often ate unhealthily prepared rations.

Between May and September 1944, while the campaign against Myitkyina was ongoing, the Chinese Army known as Y-Force finally acted. This force had been trained in Yunnan province by US instructors and armed (to a limited extent) by the Americans. Chiang Kai-shek had previously refused to allow Y-Force to be used in Burma, in protest at the lack of arms deliveries to them. On 9 May 1944 General Wei Li-huang's 72,000 men began to cross the Salween river. When they moved into Burma they were faced by only 15,000 men of the Japanese 56th Division. They fought a limited campaign in eastern Burma, taking several border cities before withdrawing back into China after a Japanese counterattack in mid-September.

Between 9 and 11 May 1944 an advance force of 32,000 men of the Nationalist Army's Y-Force crossed the Salween river from the Chinese province of Yunnan into Burma. The majority crossed the river in 400 rubber dinghies like these, while others used bamboo rafts. They crossed at two points and then climbed the gorge that dominated both banks of the river. (*US National Archives*)

(**Opposite, above**) A Chinese Nationalist hilltop machine-gun position overlooking the Salween river in June 1943. On the opposite (western) bank of the river were Japanese Imperial Army positions. The two bitter enemies watched each other, and the standoff continued until the following year, when the US-trained Y-Force attacked. The Salween river formed the border between Japanese-occupied eastern Burma and Yunnan province in western China. Eleven divisions of the Nationalist Army which made up the 115,000-strong Y-Force were to open up a new front against the Japanese in May 1944. (*Author's Collection*)

(**Opposite, below**) A dead Japanese soldier on the battlefield on the border between Yunnan Province and Burma in 1943. The Chinese soldiers of Y-Force proved tougher than the majority of the Nationalist Army units. In previous encounters with the Chinese Army in China from 1931 the Imperial Army had shown little respect for their enemies, but they gained a grudging respect for the troops they faced in northern Burma in 1944 and 1945. (*Author's Collection*)

(**Above**) A P-40 of the US 14th Air Force patrols along the China-Burma border in 1943 in support of the airlift from and to China over the Hump. The airlift from India was taking tons of supplies to the Chinese Nationalist Army and bringing back their troops in the opposite direction. By 1943 the P-40 was virtually obsolete but fifty-six of them continued to fly against the Japanese until they could be replaced by more modern types. (*Cody Images*)

US engineers with bulldozers and trucks at work on the Ledo-Burma Road, which was built to replace the Burma Road lost when the Japanese conquered Burma in 1942. The southern end of the road in India was connected to the railway, which brought large amounts of supplies from the port of Calcutta. At the town of Ledo the supplies were transferred to fleets of US trucks. *(US National Archives)*

The Ledo-Burma Road pictured in 1944, snaking through the hills of Assam towards the Chinese border. The construction of this vital link between Ledo in India and Mong Yu in China began in December 1942, and some 28,000 engineering troops and 35,000 native labourers worked on the project, with an average of one man dying per mile in the process. Most of the US engineers working on the road were black, and served in what were still segregated units at the time. This famous stretch of road had '21 curves' to allow trucks to slowly climb the mountainous terrain. (*US National Archives*)

General Stilwell meeting Lord Louis Mountbatten, the new Supreme Commander of Allied Forces in South-East Asia, in northern Burma in 1944. There was conflict between the two men when it was mooted that the Allies should cancel all offensive actions in Burma until Germany had been defeated. The lack of available resources might have made this a logical strategic decision, but a horrified Stilwell lobbied against the plan in the USA and it was eventually aborted. (*Author's Collection*)

(**Opposite, above**) US Lieutenant Carter-Harmon pictured in front of one of the 1st Air Commando's Sikorsky YR-4B helicopters in April 1944. The 1st Air Commando was assigned six of these radical aircraft to be used in in-theatre trials. Although two of the helicopters crashed, the others saw service, largely in evacuating wounded from the jungle. The 1st Air Commando was made up of fighters, bombers, transports, gliders and other light aircraft. Some of its Mitchell B-25 medium bombers were fitted with 75mm nose cannon, whose recoil when fired momentarily stopped the aircraft in mid-flight. (*US National Archives*)

(**Opposite, below**) Men of the US 5307th Composite Unit, better known as Merrill's Marauders, take part in training in the Indian jungle before going into northern Burma. Designed to be a deep penetration unit like the Chindits, the Marauders were formed in August 1943. The ranks were filled with an exotic mixture of so-called volunteers, including Sioux Indians and Japanese Americans, known as Nisei. The initial intake also included unwilling 'volunteers', who had been duped into joining the Marauders, having been promised non-combatant duties for the rest of the war after taking part in a three-month mission. (*US Army Archives*)

A Marauder cleans the barrel of his 60mm mortar before going into action in 1944. Smaller calibre mortars like this came into their own in the jungle fighting of 1942–5 as they could accurately bring down fire on the enemy at close quarters. According to most reports, the performance of the Marauders was mixed and lack of discipline was often an issue. The Marauders were disbanded in mid-1944 and its few remaining personnel were sent to join the redesignated 5332nd Brigade. (*Author's Collection*)

(**Opposite, above**) Colonel Frank Merrill during a pre-operation conference with his officers, including a Japanese-American translator. Merrill suffered from ill-health during the war and was often unable to take field command. The relatively small contingent of US troops in Burma from 1943 to 1945 meant that the majority of the fighting was done by British, Indian and Chinese soldiers. (*US Army Archives*)

(**Opposite, below**) Colonel Merrill poses for the camera with two Japanese-American Marauders who volunteered for military service despite their community's mistreatment at the hands of the US authorities. The Japanese volunteers were known collectively as 'Nisei' and they performed a number of roles during the Burma campaign. Most importantly, they were able to translate any Imperial Army radio communications for the Marauders. Nisei gained the often-grudging respect of their comrades, proving their loyalty to the USA with actions rather than words. (*US National Archives*)

A Chinese Nationalist soldier proudly holds up his Thompson sub-machine gun (provided by the USA) to celebrate the crossing of the Tanai river in the Hukawng Valley in March 1944. He is wearing a set of khaki drill overalls over an aertex shirt issued from British stocks. A Chinese regiment operated with Merrill's Marauders during the Hukawng Valley campaign. (*Author's Collection*)

(**Opposite, above**) Two P51A Mustang fighters of the US 1st Air Commando fly over the jungles of Burma. The Mustang in the background is being flown by Colonel Philip Cochrane, the commander of the 1st Air Commando. His unit was formed to provide air support for the Chindit operations and included pilots from the famous Flying Tigers. Based in the Indian state of Assam, the 1st Air Commando supported Allied forces throughout northern Burma from 1943. (*US Army Archives*)

(**Opposite, below left**) A Nationalist Chinese soldier stands guard at the Chinese end of the Burma Road in 1944. He is wearing a scruffy wadded cotton uniform and a French Adrian helmet, and compares poorly with his X-Force compatriots. Few Chinese troops were to receive the kind of training that the Nationalist units in India and western China benefited from between 1942 and 1944. (*Author's Collection*)

(**Opposite, below right**) Chinese Nationalist troops trudge along the monsoon-affected track, which has turned into a quagmire. The two soldiers in the foreground are carrying their kit on poles to disperse the weight. Both are wearing khaki drill summer uniforms with shorts and shirts that would have been inadequate for the conditions they faced. (*Author's Collection*)

A Nationalist Chinese radio operator in a jungle
clearing tries to contact his divisional headquarters. The
training that the Chinese personnel of X-Force received
at the Indian training facilities at Ramgarh included
courses in both signalling and radio operation. Few
Nationalist units in mainland China had sophisticated
communications equipment like this radio set supplied
by the USA. (*Author's Collection*)

General Sun Li-jen, the enigmatic commander of the
Nationalist 38th Division, was one of the best Chinese
officers in the Second World War. Sun had attended
the renowned Virginia Military Institute in the USA and
had commanded troops in the 1942 campaign. He
earned the respect of his allies, including General
Stilwell, who had little time for most of the Nationalist
Army's commanders. (*Author's Collection*)

Japanese machine-gunners defend their position during the fighting in northern Burma in 1944. The Japanese had fought to hold back the advance of the joint Chinese-US force through the mountains and valleys of northern Burma since February 1944. Soldiers of the Imperial 18th Division managed to delay the Allies' progress through the Hukawng and Mogaung valleys, and also faced them in the mountains of the Kumon range to the north-west of the Allied objective of Myitkyina. (*Author's Collection*)

A Chinese Nationalist soldier fires from cover using a P-17 rifle, issued to him by the USA. Although the P-17 was largely phased out of US service apart from as a sniper's rifle, it was still a serviceable weapon. His uniform is a mixture of US and British, with an M2 steel helmet and Indian Army issue pullover. Most US instructors admired their Chinese pupils' hardiness, but were frustrated by some of the bad habits they brought with them from Nationalist service. (*Author's Collection*)

(**Opposite, above**) Nationalist machine-gunners of Stilwell's X-Force fire their Browning M1917 A1 medium machine gun at Japanese positions in northern Burma. Soldiers like these had received good training in India, and their discipline and morale were much higher than the average Chinese soldier's. The Japanese refused to believe that the same Chinese whom they had defeated repeatedly since 1937 could now match them man for man. (*Author's Collection*)

(**Opposite, below**) Chinese Nationalist troops bring in Japanese prisoners during the fighting in northern Burma in 1944. The Chinese are dressed in a cross-section of British and US uniforms, and have equipment from these sources. Japanese prisoners were highly prized for the information they could give to intelligence officers. The horrific actions of Japanese troops in China from the early 1930s meant that any such prisoners would be lucky to receive good treatment from their captors. (*Author's Collection*)

(**Above**) Private Koo Ho-king, a Nationalist boy-soldier. The journalist who took the photograph was told that Koo was 7 years old and served in the 39th Division of the New 6th Army, which was fighting along the Burma Road in July 1944. Such boy-soldiers were often adopted by Nationalist units, and spent most of the time acting as helpers for their adult comrades. (*Author's Collection*)

A rare photograph showing Japanese troops of the 18th Division moving through the jungles of northern Burma in 1944. The garrison of the vital town of Myitkyina fought hard against the US-Chinese forces that besieged them from May to August, holding out against superior Allied troops in what was to prove a classic example of resolute defence. On 3 August, after a 79-day siege and acting under orders from General Mizukami, Colonel Fusayasu Maruyama evacuated Myitkyina, and managed to get 600 men of the garrison safely across the Irrawaddy river. *(Author's Collection)*

In what some would regard as a distasteful photograph, four Merrill's Marauders pose behind the bodies of Japanese soldiers they have just killed. The brutal fighting in Burma led to many on the Allied side developing a dark humour, which was unsurprising in the circumstances. Marauders gained a mixed reputation in their early operations, with some commentators saying they were ill-disciplined. Some of the Marauders were bitter, believing they had been tricked by the Army into volunteering. They were promised a short but hard operational period of service, to be followed by easy postings for the rest of the war, but this promise was soon forgotten as the Army reneged on the deal. (*US National Archives*)

(**Above**) A patrol of Merrill's Marauders moves through the Burmese jungle during the advance on the Japanese-held town of Myitkina. They are armed with a mixture of M2 carbines and an M1 Garand rifle, while the man bringing up the rear has a Thompson sub-machine gun. The Marauders always travelled as lightly as possible and dressed in as comfortable a uniform as they could. During the opening phase of the advance on the vital base, the Marauders advanced on the left flank of the Chinese Nationalist 38th Division. After moving through the Hukawng Valley, they marched through the Kumon mountains to attack the Japanese airfield at Nhpumga. (*US Army Archives*)

(**Opposite, above**) The crew of a US 37mm anti-tank gun fires at a Japanese pillbox on the outskirts of the town of Myitkina in mid-May 1944. Operations by Chinese and US forces finally saw the fall of the vital town in the first days of August 1944. Because of poor intelligence security in the theatre Stilwell had only told General Slim about the possibility of capturing the town. He did not tell Chinese Nationalist commanders as he did not trust them to observe the confidentiality he wanted. (*Cody Images*)

(**Opposite, below**) Wounded US soldiers are brought in by bullock cart to be evacuated from the recently captured Myitkyina air strip. C-47 Dakotas, seen here in the background, would take them to the military hospitals in India. During the siege of Myitkyina, which ended in August 1944, the Marauders suffered 2,207 casualties. The siege proved to be their swan song, and the force was disbanded shortly afterwards. (*US National Archives*)

A mule supply column of Chinese Nationalist soldiers of the 22nd Division on the vital Ledo Road in early August 1944. The newly built road was becoming the main land route between India and China. Chiang Kai-shek's troops under Stilwell's command were to fight their own successful campaign in north-east Burma over the next year. (*Author's Collection*)

Chapter Seven

The Second Arakan Campaign: Operation Ha-Go 1943–4

In late 1943 the western Burmese region of Arakan was proposed as the site for a new offensive by both the 14th Army and the Japanese. The British 15th Corps, made up of the 5th and 7th Indian Divisions, was stationed at Cox's Bazaar on the Arakan-India border and the troops had been undergoing jungle training in order that they would be better prepared for the coming offensive in Arakan. The 15th Corps began advancing at a slow pace towards Arakan in November 1943, with its main objectives being the ports along the Arakan coast, which could then be used to supply any future offensives from India into northern and central Burma. The 5th and 7th Indian Divisions moved into the Mayu Peninsula, with the 5th advancing down the right side of the Mayu mountain range that runs down the centre of the peninsula, and the 7th on the left side. Another division, the 81st West African, was to protect their eastern flank; this division was to be supplied by air as it was too far away from the 14th Army's supply lines. The port of Maungdaw was captured in January but British intelligence had received information about a potential Japanese offensive into India, which was to be preceded by a smaller offensive, Operation Ha-Go, in Arakan. Ha-Go was intended to draw the 14th Army's forces away from the India-Burma border in an attempt to assist the larger Japanese offensive, Operation U-Go (see Chapters 8 and 9). Both sides regarded the operations in Arakan as a sideshow to the main events around the India-Burma border, which began a few months later.

On 4 February the Japanese 55th Division under the command of Major General Sakurai counterattacked against the 15th Corps. The Japanese split their forces into four columns, with one column designated to attack the 15th Corps headquarters. In command of the assault force, however, was Colonel S. Tanahasi, leading his 'Tanahasi Column'. The Japanese advance was aimed mainly at the 15th Corps supply and administrative centre at Sinzweya, known as the 'Admin Box'. Sinzweya, located in a natural depression about a mile wide by a mile and a half long, was situated at the eastern end of the strategic Ngakyedauk Pass. Surrounded by jungle-clad hills, the

Admin Box was very vulnerable to attack, with the defenders having few places in which to shelter from the coming Japanese assault. It was garrisoned by units of the 7th Indian Division and lay 6 miles from the Arakan coastline. The Admin Box was quickly surrounded by 8,000 troops of the 55th Division with a large number of mortars and a few 105mm and 70mm guns. From 12 February the garrison of 2,500 men were wholly reliant on air support for their supplies, with all land routes cut off by the Japanese. The limited numbers of first-line troops in the garrison comprised two companies of the 2nd West Yorkshire Regiment, six batteries of artillery with a total of twenty field guns, and a unit of the Gurkha Rifles. Also at Sinzweya were two squadrons of Lee medium tanks belonging to the 25th Dragoons. Without the same level of support, the besieging Japanese force soon began to run out of supplies. At the height of the battle the Japanese captured a Sinzweya dressing station and killed all the doctors and patients in a gruesome fashion. The attacks on the Admin Box became increasingly desperate, with the Japanese launching repeated and costly bayonet charges. After seventeen days of heavy fighting the Japanese were starving and they began to withdraw from the Admin Box having lost 5,000 men. From 24 February the Sinzweya garrison began to link up with other Indian units and launched a counterattack in early March. Its success left the remains of the 55th Division cut off in the western Arakan and by June those who could had left the region. Meanwhile the Allied success meant that the 5th and 7th Indian Divisions could be transferred to fight at Imphal.

(**Opposite, above**) A Lancashire Fusilier aims his Thompson M1928 sub-machine gun from behind the shelter of a tree. He is giving covering fire to his comrades who are outflanking the village, which was probably held by a unit of Japanese troops. A battalion of Fusiliers was part of the 77th Brigade, which formed the elite of Wingate's Chindit force in 1944. (*Author's Collection*)

(**Opposite, below**) Indian troops move across open ground during the fighting in Arakan in 1944, with local volunteers seen in the distance. In the foreground of the photograph lies a dead soldier of the Imperial Army, killed in the firefight that had just ended. Japanese losses in the battle for the Admin Box were 5,000 killed, with another 2,000 killed in the fighting that followed. (*Cody Images*)

(**Above**) Soldiers of the 7th Indian Division take up a defensive position in the Ngakyedauk Pass as the Japanese 55th Division advanced in February 1944. The 55th's initial target was the 7th Division's poorly defended headquarters at Sinzweya, commonly known as the 'Admin Box', situated at the eastern end of the pass. The battle for Sinzweya was to go down in history as one of the epic actions of the Second World War. (*Cody Images*)

(**Opposite, above left**) A heavily camouflaged Japanese soldier sprints forward during an attack on British positions. The Japanese were experts in covert tactics and were specially trained in how to infiltrate enemy positions. Japanese troops sometimes mimicked British voices as they approached Allied trenches in an attempt to confuse the already nervous enemy. Some suicide troops approached Allied positions dressed in British uniforms and then blew themselves up when they got within range of the enemy. (*Author's Collection*)

(**Opposite, above right**) An Indian soldier poses next to a straw dummy which was made by the Japanese to try to fool the Allied troops during the Arakan campaign. The Japanese were adept at various military fieldcraft skills and used any advantages that the jungle offered them. It was hoped that Allied soldiers would open fire on dummies like this and thus give away their positions to Japanese snipers. (*Author's Collection*)

(**Opposite, below**) A British tommy-gunner scans the undergrowth from his vantage point on the perimeter of the Admin Box. The fight for the admin box was one of the fiercest of the entire Burma campaign. Facing Colonel Tanahashi's 6,000-strong regiment was a small garrison comprising small units from various regiments and administrative staff. This soldier wears the India pattern pullover which was worn over a jungle green or khaki drill shirt. (*Author's Collection*)

A US-made Vultee Vengeance A-31 dive-bomber of the Royal Air Force is made ready to go on a mission in March 1944. During the 1944 Arakan campaign two RAF squadrons, the 84th and the 45th, as well as the Indian Air Force's 7th and 8th Squadrons, flew Vengeances. They were armed with four bombs, with two 500lb bombs carried in their bomb bay and with a 250lb bomb under each wing. By 1944 the Vengeance was being replaced by more modern aircraft but it continued in service until 1945. *(Author's Collection)*

Gun crew from the 2nd West Yorkshire Regiment have stripped to the waist as they man their 3-in mortar to cover the advance of their comrades in Arakan. They were taking part in a running battle just to the north of the port of Maungdaw on the Naf river. The port fell to the British on 6 January 1944 after the Japanese had evacuated their garrison.

(Author's Collection)

A Japanese machine-gunner carries the stand for his Type 92 weapon during the fighting in Arakan in early 1944. He is wearing typical tropical uniform, including an M32 helmet with a canvas cover on it. Over his shoulders he is carrying the various pieces of kit needed to keep his machine gun operable in the humid conditions of the Burmese jungle. (*Cody Images*)

The business end of a 6.5mm Type 3 medium machine gun, manned by two Japanese soldiers. The Type 3 was an underpowered and outdated design (it dated back to 1914) based on the French Hotchkiss machine gun. It was planned to replace this model with the Type 92 but this was unachievable owing to the constraints on Japanese industry. According to the training manuals, the Type 3 should have had a much larger crew, including several men supplying the feeder with its 30-round ammunition strips. (*Author's Collection*)

An Indian sniper, Hakim Beg of the 2/7th Rajput Regiment, poses proudly for the news cameraman with his Lee Enfield .303 rifle. As in other armies, the best shots were often put forward for sniper training to combat their Japanese counterparts. Japanese snipers favoured firing from trees, which they often tied themselves to and covered themselves with foliage. (*Author's Collection*)

Soldiers of the 11th East African Division from the British colony of Tanganyika are seen on the road to Kalewa in Arakan. Although the road they are travelling on is making the going relatively easy, they were to face much worse. After fighting in the Myttha Gorge against heavy Japanese resistance, the 11th captured Kalewa on 2 December 1944.

(Author's Collection)

West African troops of the 81st Division cross a river in a collapsible boat carrying their kit on their heads. The terrain in Arakan where the 81st was fighting was so difficult that sometimes even mules could not be used. These troops captured the village of Mowdok in the Sangu Valley on 8 October 1944. (*Author's Collection*)

A grinning West African soldier of the 81st African Division shows off his war trophy, an M32 Japanese steel helmet. For racial reasons the Japanese were not impressed with the British employment of West and East African troops. The Japanese propaganda announcer known as 'Tokyo Rose' called them 'cannibals' and said they were led by 'European fanatics'. (*Author's Collection*)

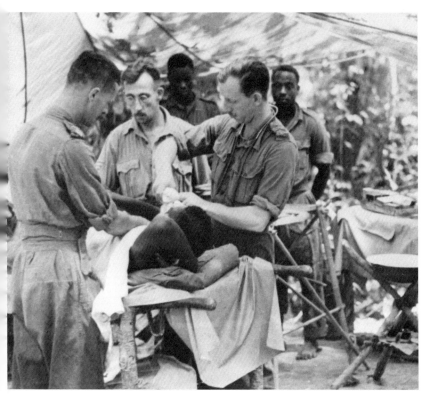

Doctors treat casualties from the 81st West African Division during the monsoon in August 1944. The 81st spent most of the monsoon season in the wild country high in the hills above the Kaladan river. Although the Africans were said to have hated Burma more than their European and Indian cousins, they were described by their officers as stoic. One officer said: 'They squatted down in their trenches, polished the leather charms they wore next to their skin, prayed to Allah for his protection and good-humouredly got on with the job.' (*Author's Collection*)

In an obviously posed propaganda photograph, Indian and African troops enjoy each other's company during a lull in the fighting. The contribution of Indian and West and East Africans in the Burma campaign cannot be overstated. Thirteen Indian divisions fought in Burma from 1943 to 1945, while two divisions of West Africans and one of East Africans also took part. (*Author's Collection*)

(**Above**) The crew of a Bofors 40mm anti-aircraft gun scan the skies as a C-47 Dakota transport plane drops supplies to the 11th East African Division. These newly arrived East African troops had taken over from the 23rd Indian Division, which was shipped back to India for rest and refitting. East African soldiers gained a fine reputation for their bush skills and their expertise in jungle patrolling. Rumours spread amongst the Japanese that the African troops filed down their teeth in order to bite their enemies! (*Cody Images*)

(**Opposite, above**) Indian soldiers about to move forward from cover in the early morning during the fighting in Arakan in 1944. The Japanese plan to draw British troops from the coming battlegrounds in northern Burma to reinforce their comrades in Arakan failed. Japanese troops had been told that if they died 'their bodies would rot, but they would turn to grass which would sway in the breezes blowing from Japan'. (*Author's Collection*)

(**Opposite, below**) In the aftermath of a Japanese ambush, a pair of Lee medium tanks and their infantry escort prepare to defend themselves from further attacks. The original caption to the photograph says: 'A short sharp action led to the annihilation of the Japanese.' These out-of-date medium tanks may have been obsolete in other theatres where they faced German tanks, but they were still useful in South-East Asia against the lightly armoured tanks and tankettes of the Imperial Army. (*Author's Collection*)

A Fox Moth biplane prepares to take off with a wounded soldier from a newly built airstrip at Kwazon, close to Taung Bazaar in Arakan. This obsolete trainer, which could take off and land on a basic airstrip, was useful in the role of a light ambulance plane. Other light planes used in this role in Burma included the US Stinson L1 and L5 and the Tiger Moth biplane. Air supply was crucial during the 1944 Arakan campaign, with 3,000 sorties flown by RAF planes delivering 10,000 tons of supplies. (*Author's Collection*)

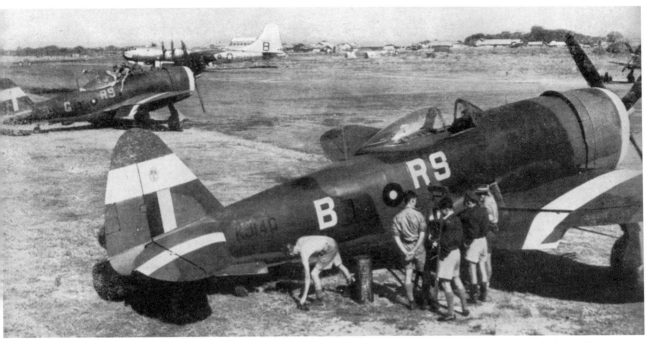

A pair of RAF Thunderbolt P-47 fighters sitting on the runway at an air base during the Arakan campaign. These fighters belonged to the 905th Wing, which was made up of four squadrons of Thunderbolts. All the aircraft flying in support of the 14th Army were under the control of the 221st Group but these fighters were still under the old 224th Group. In the background of the photograph can be seen a B-29 Flying Fortress heavy bomber, a type which flew out of bases in India. (*Author's Collection*)

Five Landing Craft Assault (LCA) boats move down-river during the Arakan campaign, which had begun on 12 December 1944. The constant shortage of river craft, especially landing craft, was a major problem for the 15th Corps of the 14th Army operating in Arakan. General Christison somehow gathered together 600 craft for his offensive, including many boats that should have been transferred to the European theatre. These were considered as too 'clapped out' to be sent back to the west but were still used in Burma until the end of the war. (*Author's Collection*)

A flotilla of Allied landing craft engaged in a supply run up a river in Arakan in an effort to keep their troops supplied. The logistics nightmare in Burma meant that any form of available transport had to be utilised. It was only the shortage of suitable river craft like these that stopped the Allies from fully using the river network. Unfortunately for the 14th Army, these craft were prioritised for the fighting in Europe and those that were kept in the Far East were often worn out. (*Author's Collection*)

Chapter Eight

The March on Delhi:
Kohima and Imphal

Although the Chindits' Operation Longcloth in 1943 was regarded as a strategic disappointment, it was certainly a propaganda victory for the Allies. One result of the operation was to awaken the Japanese Imperial Army in Burma to the possibility of a large-scale Allied offensive from India in 1944. Working on the assumption that the best form of defence is attack, the Japanese planned from early 1944 to launch a pre-emptive offensive into India. It would be launched in mid-March at the earliest, and it was a huge gamble for the Imperial Army.

The commander of the Japanese 15th Army in Burma, Lieutenant General Renya Mutaguchi, was an advocate for an offensive against India but his superior, Lieutenant General Kawabe, in command of the Burma Area Army, was not keen on the plan, which he saw as too risky. Fortunately for Mutaguchi, Kawabe's own superiors at the Southern Expeditionary Army Group HQ in Singapore were in favour of his plan. Some there were not wholly confident about the outcome of the proposed offensive but the powers that be in Tokyo were ready to approve it. Another influence on the Japanese in Burma was the presence of the Indian Nationalist leader Subhas Chandra Bose, who wanted his Indian National Army to join in the offensive to 'liberate' their homeland as they advanced into India. In reality, the Japanese had little interest in freeing the Indians from British rule, but if it helped the war effort then they were ready to exploit Bose and his INA.

The Japanese forces available for Operation U-Go – the advance through northern Burma and into India – came from the 15th Army. The 85,000-strong 15th Army had three infantry divisions (the 15th, 31st and 33rd) and was backed by 7,000 men of the 1st Division of the Indian National Army. Although these forces were substantial, there were many weaknesses in the Japanese offensive capability. One particular weakness was the lack of artillery, with the Japanese guns outnumbered 4:1 by the 14th Army's artillery arm. Similarly, the number of tanks available to Mutaguchi was insufficient. He only had the 14th Armoured Regiment, equipped with sixty-six tanks, but nearly all of them were light vehicles like the Type 94 and 97. Air cover was also going to be poor, with the RAF and USAF having gained air superiority over the Japanese in Burma. One of Mutaguchi's main weaknesses was his refusal to see the significance of Allied air superiority for the coming offensive.

The main objective for the U-Go offensive was the major Allied base at Imphal, which had been vital to the Allied war effort since mid-1942. It was the capital of the Indian state of Manipur and lay some 50 miles from the Burma-India border. It was also the HQ of the 14th Army's 4th Corps, with 120,000 men made up of the 17th, 20th and 23rd Indian Divisions covering a 250-mile front. Imphal and its large stores of supplies was regarded by the Japanese as a storehouse for the 15th Army. As they could not hope to transport enough supplies themselves, they hoped to replenish their stocks from what they hoped to capture at Imphal. A secondary objective for the offensive was the administrative base at Kohima, 80 miles to the north of Imphal in the trackless region known as Nagaland. It was the residence of a District Commissioner, but more importantly it stood on the road between Imphal and the main railhead at the northern city of Dimapur, 130 miles to the north.

Slim's plan was to allow the 15th Army to advance across northern Burma, extending their increasingly precarious supply lines. Imphal and Kohima would then be well supplied by air and, if possible, reinforced during the expected long battle. Within weeks Slim knew that the Japanese forces besieging the two 14th Army strongholds would run out of food and ammunition. If the garrisons of Imphal and Kohima could hold out, then a wholesale Japanese defeat was almost inevitable.

Mountain artillery crewmen of the 15th Imperial Army take part in pre-offensive training in northern Burma in the spring of 1944. There were five artillery regiments involved in the Kohima-Imphal Offensive, two of which were equipped with Type 94 75mm guns like these. In the coming offensive the Japanese were to be totally outgunned, with only 90 field pieces compared to the Allies' 330. (*Author's Collection*)

During the build-up to the launch of the U-Go offensive a Japanese signaller sends a message to a nearby unit in the hills of northern Burma. Allied reconnaissance and intelligence missions had seen evidence that the Imperial Army was preparing for a major attack, with air reconnaissance spotting Japanese engineers improving the roads leading from central Burma to the Chindwin river. In addition, it had been seen that the Japanese were collecting boats that could be used to get their troops across the Chindwin. (*Author's Collection*)

Lieutenant General Renya Mutaguchi, commander of the 15th Imperial Army, pictured before the war. Mutaguchi was the main advocate for the planned offensive in northern Burma and into the Indian states of Manipur and Assam. There had been talks in Japanese circles about extending the war into India since the end of the conquest of Burma in mid-1942. Initial plans for the offensive were dusted down and updated as the Japanese realised they had to do something to turn around their fading fortunes. Mutaguchi had to persuade some of his fellow generals about the feasibility of the offensive but his over-optimistic zeal rubbed off on most of them. (*Author's Collection*)

(**Opposite, above**) During the build-up to the launch of the U-Go offensive the Japanese launched a number of aggressive patrols to test out the preparedness of British and Indian positions. Here, officers check their map – although maps were notoriously inaccurate – to try to gather more information for the forthcoming attack. The Japanese had spent the early twentieth century gathering intelligence for their long-planned war against the Western Powers. However, the conquest of Burma had never really been part of the plans of the Japanese High Command before 1941. (*Author's Collection*)

(**Opposite, below**) The senior officers of the 15th Army pose for a group photograph before the launch of the U-Go offensive at Mutaguchi's HQ at Maymyo. Seated in the front row (*left to right*) are Generals Yanagida, Tanaka, Mutaguchi, Matsuyame and Sato. There was a level of disagreement between the various commanders over launching the offensive in the first place but once they were committed to it, all the commanders did their best to make the risky venture a success. (*Author's Collection*)

(**Above**) Japanese 15th Army troops move through hilly country en route to the British base at Imphal, with its much sought-after stores. The Imperial Army could cover huge distances on foot and its soldiers were described as walking rather than marching. Unlike in other armies, Japanese soldiers were allowed to drink from their canteens wherever they wanted. They were often unshaven and had their jacket or shirt buttons undone; smartness on campaign was not a priority. Nevertheless, they lacked little when it came to soldiering and for much of the Burma campaign they were regarded as jungle supermen. (*Author's Collection*)

During training for the Imphal Offensive, this 3-in mortar crew of the Indian National Army rehearse their firing drill. The INA units involved in the 1944 fighting were dressed in ex-British khaki drill uniforms and armed with former British rifles, machine guns and artillery. But when the fighting began, the heavy weaponry had to be left behind and they had to fight with small arms only. (*Cody Images*)

(**Opposite, above**) The crew of a 150mm Type 96 howitzer fire their gun towards British positions at the start of the U-Go offensive. The Type 96 was heavier than its predecessor (the Type 4) but it could be towed by one of the four types of artillery half-tracks in service. Unfortunately for the Japanese there was a shortage of these tractors available to the Imperial Army in 1944. (*Author's Collection*)

(**Opposite, below**) The crew of this Type 94 75mm mountain gun aim across the Imphal Plain towards the foothills of the Naga and Chindwin Hills. These light guns were the only ones that could practically be moved through the terrain facing the 15th Army in March 1944. An almost total lack of motor vehicles, especially artillery tractors, meant that these guns had to be dragged by men and mules up the hills of northern Burma. (*Cody Images*)

殺然たり凜然たりビルマの
新防人。防衛軍幹部候補生

(**Opposite, above**) An Indian National Army armoured column takes part in training for their participation in the 'liberation' of their motherland. The INA had an armoured unit made up of ex-British Bren gun carriers like this vehicle and Marmon-Herrington armoured cars. Like all the other weaponry and equipment used by the INA, these worn-out armoured vehicles had been captured during the Japanese victory in 1941–2. (*Author's Collection*)

(**Opposite, below**) The crew of this 3.7-in pack howitzer of the British Army take part in drill in their artillery position in February 1944. Within a few weeks gun crews like this would be facing the advance of the Imperial Japanese Army. This gun has been modernised with the addition of pneumatic tyres in place of the original wooden ones. Originally regarded as an infantry support gun, from 1932 it was replaced in that role by the 3-in mortar. It was, however, still in service in 1939 and was to serve in Burma until the end of the campaign. (*Author's Collection*)

(**Left**) A Burmese National Army recruit pictured during training for a potential role in the coming campaign against the British on the Indo-Burmese border. Although the inclusion of BNA units in the Imphal offensive was discussed by the Japanese, there were worries about their reliability. In the end these worries outweighed the desperate need for more men for the offensive and no Burmese fought in the 1944 campaign. (*Author's Collection*)

(**Above**) Japanese light artillerymen prepare their 75mm Type 94 mountain gun, which they have camouflaged with foliage to merge into the jungle. They have also fastened fronds from the same trees to their helmets and their shoulders to make it harder for the enemy to spot their position. The lighter guns used by the Imperial Army usually broke down into sections so that their crews could move them around by hand. (*Author's Collection*)

(**Opposite**) General Sir George J. Giffard, commander-in-chief of the 11th Army Group in South-East Asia, talks to soldiers at Imphal. He had taken over the role from General Irwin, who had been sacked in the aftermath of the first Arakan campaign in 1943. The many changes in the command structure in South-East Asia and especially in Burma resulted in a more efficient Allied army. (*Author's Collection*)

Soldiers of an Indian Army unit prepare to go out on patrol around Imphal in the build-up to the main Japanese assault. Indian troops followed several religions and supplying the Muslims, Hindus and Sikhs with their dietary requirements was difficult. Hindu soldiers could not eat standard ration bully beef and were issued instead with extra milk and clarified butter. (Author's Collection)

A disabled Type 97 tankette of the Imperial Army is towed from the road where it was destroyed in fighting at Tamu, 30 miles south-east of Imphal. This type of light tank was armed with a 37mm main gun. This one was destroyed by soldiers of the 23rd Indian Division, which had been sent to defend Tamu. There were few Japanese tanks available in Burma in 1944 and most, like this lightly armoured and poorly armed model, were soon destroyed.
(Author's Collection)

British 4th Corps troops advance across the Imphal Plain to take up defensive positions as the Japanese Imperial Army advances northwards towards them. Their commander, General Slim, wanted to entice the Japanese forces to extend their precarious supply lines. He hoped that the Japanese would wear themselves out in repeated attacks against the well dug-in Allied garrisons at Kohima and Imphal. (*Author's Collection*)

Chapter Nine

Japanese Defeat: Kohima and Imphal 1944

At the start of the Japanese offensive into India in the spring of 1944, Lieutenant General Renya Mutaguchi, the 15th Imperial Army commander, made a long speech to his men, in which he claimed that 'The army has now reached the state of invincibility, and the day when the Rising Sun shall proclaim our definite victory in India is not far off.' He carried on in the same vein, telling his men that victory was assured, but it is doubtful whether he truly believed this himself.

When the great northern offensive, Operation U-Go, began, Mutaguchi chose to control it remotely from his HQ at Maymyo hundreds of miles from the front. His hope was that victory would be achieved before Emperor Hirohito's birthday on 29 April. One sign of confidence among the Japanese commanders was the order that 'comfort women' – sex slaves – were to be flown into Imphal ten days after the offensive began. On 15 March Mutaguchi ordered the 31st Infantry Division to cross the Chindwin river and strike for Kohima. It took two weeks of struggling through dense jungle for the Japanese to reach the perimeter of Kohima. Late March saw the Japanese enveloping the Kohima garrison, with little opposition from the defenders who were busy preparing their defences. It now became plain to the Japanese officers that the road to the vital supply bases at Dimapur, 46 miles from Kohima, was undefended. Mutaguchi passed on this information to his superior, Kawabe, and suggested his men should bypass Kohima and attack Dimapur instead. Kawabe insisted that he obey his orders to take Kohima first. In the meantime the 14th Army had sent reinforcements to Dimapur and the best chance for the Japanese to win the battle was lost. By early April the Japanese had succeeded in cutting off the Kohima garrison from a relief column trying to move up from Dimapur. Kohima's 3,000-strong garrison included a number of administrative staff, who had had only the most basic of training. The rest consisted of the 4th Battalion, Queen's Own Royal West Kent Regiment, soldiers of the Assam Regiment and one regiment of Nepalese troops. They were expecting an attack by three Japanese battalions, not the whole of the Imperial 31st Division. The first assault on the base took place on 5 April with a night attack by the 58th Regiment. On the following day the West Kents launched a counterattack but were beaten back. Over the next fourteen days the Japanese 58th and 138th Regiments repeatedly attacked the gradually shrinking perimeter of Kohima, supported by seventeen Type 94 mountain guns that had been dragged over the hills to their positions. In the bunkers and trenches of Kohima the often hand-to-hand fighting was desperate, with the RAF dropping supplies in pinpoint air-drops to the defenders. As long as the defenders could hold on, and the air-drops continued, then the Japanese were almost certain to fail. They were running out of food and ammunition as their tenuous supply lines failed, largely due to the conditions created by the monsoon. As their casualties mounted, the odds against the Japanese rose to five to one, and they were literally starving to death. The Japanese commander received orders to continue the increasingly hopeless attacks on Kohima. He answered Mutaguchi by saying: 'The 15th Army has failed to send me supplies and ammunition since the operation began! That failure releases me from any obligation to obey orders!' Relief forces made up of the 2nd, 4th and 7th Indian Divisions were applying increasing pressure on the Japanese forces at Kohima. Despite the continuing air-drops, the garrison was also in desperate straits, each man having to survive on a pint of water a day. The besieging Japanese had run out of all medical supplies and were reported to be eating grass. While the battle for Kohima was coming to its inevitable conclusion, the struggle for Imphal was under way.

Mutaguchi had designated 7 March as D-day for Operation U-Go. He had under his command the 15th, 31st and 33rd Infantry Divisions totalling 85,000 men, with an additional 7,000 Indian National Army volunteers. Mutaguchi was confident of victory even though he only had one field gun for every four that the 14th Army had. His 114th Armoured Regiment, made up mainly of outdated light tanks, would be faced by 120 Lee-Grant and Sherman tanks of the 254th Armoured Brigade. He also knew that his men only had 20 days' worth of supplies, but he was sure that they could replenish their stocks from the storehouses they would capture at Imphal. The Japanese advanced along a 150-mile front in nine large columns. There was little motor transport, and their few trucks could only move at night owing to Allied air superiority. Instead, Japanese transport relied on 17,000 pack animals, mainly horses and mules. Mutaguchi reportedly believed that most animals could be utilised as pack animals, including goats, elephants and cows. Reportedly 15,000 cows had been trained as pack animals, but they were not used during the campaign. There were even stories that the cows and bullocks were to be dyed green! At first, the advance went surprisingly well, with the nine columns pushing aside any opposition and thrusting through jungle, across rivers and over mountains.

When the British saw the extent of the U-Go offensive, they pulled back the troops stationed around Imphal and brought them inside the perimeter. General Slim ordered that the 5th Indian Division should be airlifted into Imphal, and also made sure that reinforcements began to move up to the front. On 29 March the Japanese 15th Division cut the Imphal-Kohima road and by 6 April the combined 15th and 33rd Divisions had cut off Imphal. The Imphal garrison was made up of the 5th and 17th Indian Divisions, the 50th Parachute Brigade and the 254th Tank Brigade. These units were now defending a large 20-mile wide perimeter, with orders to hold their ground and let the Japanese wear themselves out by launching repeated assaults. The garrison had withdrawn into their positions in good order and were receiving regular supplies by air. Despite their best efforts, the Japanese could not push the garrison out of Imphal, although a number of strongholds changed hands during the fighting. By 13 April the Japanese attacks had begun to lose their impetus largely due to the irregular supplies they were receiving. Once their initial supplies had run out, the Japanese soldiers quickly began to starve. Despite pleas sent to Mutaguchi from various Japanese unit commanders at the front, the situation did not improve. When one of his commanders complained that his men did not have enough to eat, he was immediately sacked by Mutaguchi. Throughout April and into early May the British forces managed to defend the long Imphal perimeter against constant Japanese attacks. Japanese losses during the desperate frontal attacks against the British positions were unsustainable. One 3,000-strong regiment of the 33rd Division had been reduced to only 800 men by April. Japanese morale began to suffer and small numbers of troops began to desert their positions and go over to the British lines.

Both sides were totally exhausted by early May. On the Japanese side, only the 33rd Division was receiving regular supplies but even these ended later that month. The other two divisions were getting some ammunition but very little food, and their soldiers were starving to death. If things were bad for the Japanese, their Indian allies in the INA were in an even worse situation. Indian National Army volunteers had been left to their own devices by their erstwhile allies and were starving in large numbers. The morale of the INA had been high when they crossed onto 'sacred' Indian soil in Manipur but hunger soon saw morale slump as the reality of their situation dawned on them. They began to die in large numbers. Instead of taking Imphal as planned in April, the fighting went on and the Japanese supply lines were inadequate to keep so many troops in the field. If the weather was good, trucks could move up to the front at night but once they reached the front line the supplies could not be distributed properly. Adverse weather conditions made things very difficult for both sides, but the Japanese did not have the advantage of air supply. The pack animals that the Japanese relied on were dying in huge numbers, with the vast majority of horses and mules lost during the campaign. On 5 May the 14th Army began extensive counterattacks around Imphal but these were beaten back by ferocious Japanese defenders. During the rest of May and into June it became obvious that U-Go had failed, but no Japanese commander was ready to lose face by admitting this. This attitude was exemplified by a speech made by an officer of the

33rd who told his men at the start of Operation U-Go that they would 'face annihilation in their attack on Imphal' but they would 'win a great victory'. He also told them that their dead ancestors would be their audience when they went into battle.

Finally on 5 July their soldiers' desperate plight dawned on the Imperial Army commanders. It was obvious that maintaining the campaign around Imphal would only result in thousands more dead Japanese. The order to suspend the operation was delayed for another eight days as Mutaguchi hesitated to give the order for the 15th Army to withdraw. To add insult to injury, it took until 19 July for the order to withdraw to the Chindwin river to be acted upon by his commanders. The Japanese now had to retreat along roads made impassable by the monsoon, with many little more than rivers. When they reached the main rivers they had to cross during their withdrawal – the Yu, Manipur and Chindwin – there were few boats available to transport them. Apart from a few native boats operated by 'friendly' Burmese, rafts had to be built to get men and equipment across. As they struggled along, they discovered that the food depots that should have been provided to feed the retreating soldiers were not there. The terrible conditions and lack of food led to a breakdown of discipline in many units as survival became a matter of 'every man for himself'. Survivors of the debacle at Imphal made their way painfully back into Burma, finally leaving Indian soil by 20 August. They were followed closely by units of the 14th Army, who were 'snapping at their heels' throughout the retreat.

The Japanese losses in the fighting for Kohima and Imphal were devastating, with the original 115,000 men being reduced to 50,000. At the start of the campaign the 15th Division had a strength of 20,000 men; by the end it had 4,000. The 31st Division also started the campaign with 20,000 men but was reduced to 7,000 by the end of the fighting. The 25,000 men in the 33rd Division lost 21,000 casualties, while the 50,000 personnel in rear units had suffered 15,000 losses. British and Indian losses were also heavy, with 12,525 casualties, including 2,669 killed. In return, British and Indian units captured a hundred artillery pieces from the Japanese. Another casualty of the campaign was Mutaguchi, whose stubborn attitude and poor leadership during Operation U-Go had cost his men dearly. He was relieved of his command on 30 August, called back to Japan and was forced into retirement in December.

(**Opposite, above**) A Burmese guide points out the lie of the land to a Japanese officer close to the Burma-Indian border at the beginning of the U-Go offensive. Although the majority Burman population may have been friendly towards the Imperial Army, many minority peoples were hostile to them. Guides like this man were essential to the Japanese as their maps of the territory they were advancing into were poor. (*Author's Collection*)

(**Opposite, below**) This British machine-gun crew at Kohima is armed with a Browning M1916 medium machine gun taken from a tank. The men have tried to fortify their position with some large rocks, leaving a space to fire their gun through. Such isolated positions came under night attacks from Japanese infiltrators who tried to spook the defenders. One trick was to crawl close to British positions in the dark and call in broken English to the defenders to 'let me through' or 'the japs are after me, let me through'. (*Author's Collection*)

(**Opposite, above**) Soldiers of the 10th Gurkhas clean up their dugouts and trenches on Scraggy Hill, one of the hills that made up the Kohima defence perimeter. During the struggle for Kohima, close-quarter, hand-to-hand fighting for control of dugouts and slit trenches was ferocious. Often Japanese and Allied soldiers were eating and sleeping only yards or even feet from their enemy. One Japanese soldier who was trying to deepen his dugout was even throwing the soil from his shovel into a British trench! (*Cody Images*)

(**Opposite, below**) Jeep ambulances moving casualties to the field hospital at Kohima after the end of the siege at the town. During the battle the British and Indian garrison suffered an estimated 4,064 casualties. Confusion over the losses suffered means that the number of dead amongst the casualties is not known with certainty. Japanese losses were said to have been 5,764, with a higher proportion of fatalities owing to their almost total lack of medical facilities. (*Cody Images*)

(**Above**) A Bren gunner in an isolated British outpost in the hills above the eastern Imphal plain looks for signs of the expected Japanese advance. The 'glittering' prize for the Imperial Army was the large stocks of military and other supplies at the forward supply base at Imphal. The Japanese planned to use the captured Imphal base as its 'larder' and source of arms and ammunition. With Imphal in its hands, the Imperial Army could then move into India and secure northern Burma against Allied attacks. (*Cody Images*)

This British soldier has stopped along a jungle track to listen for any sounds of movement from the undergrowth. As the war progressed, Allied troops became more adept at reading the jungle that they had previously regarded as totally alien. Although the Japanese soldiers' reputation as good jungle fighters was well earned, by 1944 the British had also learned to operate in jungle conditions. (*Cody Images*)

The crew of a Type 92 heavy machine gun prepare to fire their weapon towards the British positions. The Allies nicknamed it the 'woodpecker' after the distinctive sound it made when fired. One British soldier stumbled into a Japanese machine-gun position in the dark and only realised when the familiar 'woodpecker' sound came from just a few feet away. (*Author's Collection*)

This propaganda photograph from the heady early days of the Imphal offensive features a Vickers heavy machine-gun crew of the Indian National Army. These Sikh volunteers had largely joined the INA in 1942 rather than going into prisoner-of-war camps where conditions were brutal. Some, however, were genuine supporters of Indian independence and fought fanatically for that cause during the 1944 fighting. (*Author's Collection*)

(**Opposite, above**) A British Army officer at Imphal sends a message back to his headquarters using his unit's radio, which is strapped to the operator's back. The terrain and atmospherics of Burma led to problems with radio transmissions at times. After dusk this natural interference got much worse and constantly disrupted and delayed radio signals. (*Cody Images*)

(**Opposite, below**) Two British officers are in the process of dismantling their radio equipment at their Imphal headquarters to move to another bunker. During the siege delicate specialist equipment like this had to be taken good care of as attempting to replace it by air-drop would have been difficult. (*Author's Collection*)

(**Above**) A US Lee medium tank crosses a river as part of the relief column that was advancing towards the embattled Imphal garrison. These tanks were obsolete in other theatres of the war and had been withdrawn from North Africa by 1943. However, with their 75mm main armament and 37mm turret gun, these tanks were still potent when faced by the poor tanks of the Imperial Army. (*Author's Collection*)

Lieutenant General Masakazu Kawabe, the 58-year-old commander-in-chief of the Japanese Burma Area Army, pictured during the war. He had been persuaded by his subordinate Mutaguchi that the Imphal campaign had a realistic chance of success but when he visited the front himself in June 1944 he soon realised that the offensive had failed and the situation was desperate for his men in northern Burma. Even so, he insisted that Mutaguchi continue his doomed campaign regardless of the consequences as the Japanese Army's honour was at stake. (*Author's Collection*)

The 5th Indian Division was airlifted to Imphal at the height of the battle, along with food supplies including cattle, like this one being loaded onto a C-47 transport. As the fighting in Arakan died down, the 5th Division was made available to bolster their comrades in north-eastern India. (*Author's Collection*)

The advance units of the 33rd and 4th Corps meet on the road linking Imphal and Kohima in June 1944. Units from the different 14th Army strongholds in Manipur state were often able to support each other as the Japanese U-Go offensive developed. As the campaign progressed into June the 14th Army gained ascendance over the struggling Japanese. This M3A3 tank belonged to the 254th Indian Tank Brigade, which was part of the Imphal defence force in 1944. (*Author's Collection*)

This photograph symbolises the abject state of the Japanese Army after the fighting in northern Burma in 1944. This 150mm Model 96 howitzer had been dragged over hills during the advance and then abandoned in the mud when the Japanese retreated. Most heavy equipment and weaponry had to be left behind as the Japanese soldiers withdrew from the horrendous conditions they had endured for months. (*Author's Collection*)

This Japanese machine-gun crew were hit by mortar fire during the heavy fighting around Imphal in March 1944. They did not survive. It is a Vickers M1912 heavy machine gun, which suggests that it belonged to the Indian National Army. Because of the desperate situation faced by the Imperial Army, some units stripped their Indian allies of any weaponry apart from rifles. (*Author's Collection*)

Allied officers clamber over a Japanese Type 97 Te-Ke light tank which was abandoned in the withdrawal from Imphal. The Type 97, with its 37mm main gun, was one of the most modern light tanks in the world when it was first produced in 1937. By 1944 it was outgunned and out-armoured, with a maximum armoured plating of 12mm. Nevertheless, with few alternatives available to the Japanese, it was to stay in service until the end of the war. (*Author's Collection*)

Subhas Chandra Bose, the Indian Nationalist leader and commander of the Indian National Army, is seen close to the front line in the summer of 1944, posing in military uniform complete with steel helmet taken from the British Army stores in Singapore in 1942. Bose had no scruples about siding with the Fascist Axis Powers in his quest for Indian independence. Having previously set up an Indian Legion in Germany he was quoted as saying 'I have travelled the world and seen the standard of the German Army: they will win!' (*Author's Collection*)

Field Marshal Earl Wavell, Viceroy of India, inspects captured Japanese small arms after the Allied victory at Imphal. Nearly all the Japanese rifles and machine guns used by the Imperial Army in 1944 had been issued in the 1920s and mid-1930s. Both types of machine gun seen here had some design faults but had to serve with the army until 1945. Some improved models of heavy and light machine guns were introduced into service but not in the numbers needed to replace the old models. (*Author's Collection*)

This poor quality and rare photograph shows stragglers from the 15th Japanese Army withdrawing from the disastrous fighting at Imphal. These demoralised soldiers are lucky to have hitched a ride in a native canoe, while their comrades wait for other boats. What little heavy equipment they had was left behind on the northern battlefields and they have only their rifles and personal kit left. (*Cody Images*)

Chapter Ten

North-Eastern Burma 1944–5

Following the fall of Myitkyina in early August 1944, the fighting in north-east Burma saw a short hiatus. In a change of formations within the Northern Combat Area Command, the British 36th Division had been flown into Myitkyina airfield to replace the Chindits who were withdrawn after Operation Thursday. General Festing, commander of the 36th Division, asked General Stilwell if he could retain the Chinese artillery that had been attached, but the request was refused. Stilwell was a well known Anglophobe, although he eventually gained respect for General Festing and his men, who in his eyes had proved their worth. At the same time Merrill's Marauders were disbanded and replaced by an expanded version known as the Mars Task Force. The surviving Marauders were absorbed into the new force.

The command position on the northern Burma front in the summer of 1944 was strained to say the least. General Stilwell was still under the orders of the Chinese Nationalist leader Chiang Kai-shek, but their relationship had been difficult for several years; indeed, Stilwell had a strong personal dislike for Chiang, which was reciprocated. In an effort to soothe this difficult relationship, in August 1944 the USA had offered the services of General Patrick Hurley to act as an intermediary. Chiang Kai-shek had threatened to remove his troops from Burma unless the level of US aid increased. In reality, Chiang was more interested in the coming civil war with the Chinese Communists than in victory in Burma. The amount of military aid he received could well swing the balance in the inevitable conflict with Chiang's main enemy, the Red Army. In September Chiang ordered Stilwell to begin an offensive southwards from Myitkyina towards the town of Bhamo, which he hoped would take the pressure off his troops fighting the Japanese across the border in western China. Stilwell refused to do so, complaining that his troops were still too exhausted after their capture of Myitkyina in August. This disobedience only served to strengthen the Chinese leader's long-standing insistence that Stilwell be replaced. On 22 October General Stilwell was recalled to the USA and his place was taken by General Wedemayer. A far more diplomatic man than Stilwell, Wedemayer was better able to deal with Chiang Kai-shek, as well as his British Allies.

In the field, US Lieutenant General Dan I. Sultan was given command of the Northern Combat Area Command. General Sultan had under his command four Chinese Nationalist divisions (the 22nd, 30th, 38th and 50th), plus the British 36th Division and the Mars Task Force. When it went into action in late 1944 the Mars Task Force had 5,000 personnel, organised into the 475th Infantry Regiment (a long-range penetration force) and the 124th (dismounted) Cavalry Regiment of the Texas National Guard. Support units included medical units, and there were two field artillery battalions, each equipped with 75mm PACK howitzers. In addition, there was a regiment of Chinese troops under the command of Brigadier General John P. Willey and a unit of irregular Kachin levies.

In mid-October British and Chinese-US forces went over to the offensive to re-establish land communications between India and China. The US-Chinese forces moved southwards from Myitkyina as far as the Katha-Shwegu-Bhamo line, meeting little or no resistance. Sultan's forces launched a three-pronged offensive southwards from Myitkyina to the Irrawaddy river. The intention was to mop up any concentrations of Japanese troops north of the river. This plan had been conceived by Stilwell before he was sacked, and General Sultan kept more or less to his predecessor's schedule.

On the left side of the offensive the Chinese 22nd Division advanced towards Bhamo, an important town on the navigable Ayeyarwady river. Bhamo had been built up by the Japanese into a well defended stronghold since early 1944. The 1,200-strong garrison was not sufficient, however, to defend the town against the approaching Allied force. On 10 November the 38th Division outflanked Japanese positions along the Taping river before penetrating the Bhamo plain, and on 14 November the 22nd Division took the town of Man Tha. The capture of the town blocked Bhamo from receiving supplies or reinforcements, and the following day all supply links to the besieged Japanese were cut. On the 15th the Chinese 38th Division cut off all other access to the town and the US 475th Infantry Regiment reinforced the 22nd Division. By 28 November the 38th Division was increasing pressure on the northern perimeter of Bhamo and the garrison asked for help. On 5 December a 3,000-strong Japanese relief force under Colonel Yamazaki tried to break through to the town but was blocked by the 90th Regiment of the Chinese 30th Division and forced to withdraw. The siege finally ended on the 15th when the garrison managed to flee through the Chinese lines and break out to the south.

The British 36th Division had moved out of its positions around Myitkyina to advance south-westwards towards the Irrawaddy river on 4 August 1944. The troops advanced along the Myitkyina-Mandalay railway and took the town of Pinbaw after a three-day battle. Another battle took place in mid-October at Namma, where the 36th ran into heavy resistance from the Japanese, supported by the Chinese 56th Division. In early November the 36th Division reached Pinwe, a vital rail and road junction. It took three weeks of heavy fighting for the 36th to overcome the stubborn Japanese defence. By the time Pinwe fell, the Japanese had lost several thousand men and all the remaining tanks they had in Burma. The 36th continued to operate in the region between Bhamo and Lashio until it was sent to take part in the 14th Army's offensive in central Burma.

January 1945 saw the Chinese 38th Division taking part in mopping-up operations in the jungle to the south of Myitkyina. On the 15th units of X-Force who had advanced from India met up with their compatriots in Y-Force from Yunnan. This unification of Chinese forces meant the strategic Ledo Road could now be completed. The same month saw the capture of the last Japanese positions along the Burma Road; by the 28th the road had been cleared and the first convoy travelled along it from India to China. Chiang Kai-shek was rapidly losing interest in the fighting in Burma, especially as his main objective – opening the Burma Road – had been achieved. In early 1945 the 22nd and 38th Divisions were sent back to China at Chiang Kai-shek's insistence to confront the Japanese offensive in Kumming province. In March Chiang Kai-shek ordered his troops to halt any further advances in Burma at Lashio, which was duly taken on the 7th. By early April Nationalist troops in Burma had begun to withdraw northwards to cross the Chinese-Burma border back into Yunnan province. For the last few months of the Burma campaign the role of the Chinese units was taken over by Burmese guerrilla forces known as Detachment 101. This special force had been organised and trained by the USA's Office of Strategic Services (OSS) from 1943 when Karen and Kachin guerrillas received training in India. In early 1945 1,500 Kachin guerrillas had volunteered to operate against the Japanese along the Burma Road. They were joined by a force of 1,500 Karen and Shan minority guerrillas, along with Gurkha and Chinese volunteers. This well armed guerrilla army was given the task of dealing with the remaining Japanese formations in eastern and south-eastern Burma until the end of the war.

(**Above**) Nationalist Chinese troops of the 38th Division fire on Japanese defensive positions in the grounds of a temple in the northern Burmese town of Bhamo. The Japanese defending the strategic town were surrounded by Chinese forces from November 1944. Although they received 3,000 reinforcements during the siege, the town fell to the Nationalist Army's 22nd and 38th Divisions on 15 December. It was a costly victory for the Nationalist troops, with a total loss of 19,000 men wounded or killed during the five-week siege. (*Author's Collection*)

(**Opposite, above**) Soldiers of the 6th Battalion, South Wales Borderers, return from a patrol to check on the defences of Pinwe in November 1944. As well as the Borderers, the 10th Battalion, Gloucester Regiment, was also involved in the ferocious battle for the town. Pinwe was a vital rail junction on the main line south to Mandalay and the Japanese were determined to defend it for as long as possible. (*Author's Collection*)

(**Opposite, below**) A private of the Royal Engineers' field company defends a jungle path recently cleared of Japanese troops close to the town of Pinwe. The jungle to the north of the town had come under heavy bombardment from the 36th Division's artillery. Although the bombardment did a good job of levelling the jungle, the fallen trees created additional obstacles for the advancing British troops. (*Author's Collection*)

(**Above**) The seven-man crew of a 25-pounder howitzer fire their gun from under the cover of camouflage netting during the battle for Pinwe in November 1944. As one crewman passes the shells to the loader of the gun on the left side, another of the crew throws the spent shell cases onto a growing pile. By late 1944 the Allies had far more guns than the Japanese, who had lost most of theirs in the fighting earlier in the year. (*Author's Collection*)

(**Opposite, above**) An Indian soldier peers into the side hatch of a Type 37 light tank on the outskirts of Pinwe in late November 1944. Pinwe's garrison was made up of the 128th Infantry Regiment, backed up by a few light tanks. The Type 37, with its 37mm gun, was of little use by this stage of the war and in any tank-vs-tank encounters they were soon put out of action. This tank was left behind by the Japanese, who lost control of Pinwe on 30 November. (*Author's Collection*)

(**Opposite, below**) A Bren gunner moves cautiously through the undergrowth close to Pinwe in November 1944. One of his most important jobs was to keep his Bren in good working order in the humid conditions of Burma. It was commonly said that an uncovered rifle left outside in the open overnight would be rusted up by morning. All equipment and weaponry was susceptible to the high humidity, with some uniforms rotting within a few weeks. (*Author's Collection*)

A patrol from the 36th Division moves through a gully near Pinwe, looking for signs of any Japanese activity. During jungle training they were taught that while on patrol the first man in the column should look ahead, while the second man checked to his right and the third man to his left; then the fourth man looked ahead and so on. Of course, the men at back of the column would check behind them in case of ambush by Japanese, who waited for the troops to pass before attacking. (*Author's Collection*)

This Nationalist soldier fighting in northern Burma in early 1945 poses with one of his unit's mules. He is an artilleryman from a 75mm PACK howitzer battery, whose guns were supplied by the USA. Nationalist Army divisions had to rely heavily on horses and mules, with an average of a thousand animals used by each division for transport. (*Author's Collection*)

On 27 January 1945 the Chinese Nationalist Army's X-Force and Y-Force met up in the jungles of northern Burma. The two soldiers here emphasise the differences in the two Allied-trained formations. On the left is a Y-Force private dressed like the average Nationalist soldier and armed with a Mauser rifle. In contrast, the X-Force NCO has been issued with a British Army uniform (with the exception of his US-issue M1 helmet). His Thompson sub-machine gun also came from US stocks, as the Americans took responsibility for supplying most of their weaponry. *(Author's Collection)*

146

An M3A3 light tank of the 1st Provisional Tank Group moves up to the front. When these tanks first went into action in Burma they were manned by mixed US and Chinese crews. As soon as the Chinese crews had proved their competency, the US crews returned to their original roles as instructors. The Chinese were sometimes criticised for holding back in combat, but it was not through lack of bravery: in combat they were loath to risk their 'precious' tanks, which they were amazed to have been given by the USA. (*Author's Collection*)

(**Opposite, above**) A Chinese Nationalist Army's artillery team pull their ex-Russian 4.5-in howitzer along a jungle road in north-eastern Burma. These guns had been supplied to the Tsarist Russian army in the First World War and then sent to the Chinese by the Soviet Union in the 1930s. By April 1945 the Nationalist Army was being pulled back from Burma into China to help fight the Communists there. (*Author's Collection*)

(**Opposite, below**) This fine study shows the five-man crew of a Sherman M4 medium tank from the Nationalist Army's 1st Provisional Tank Group during the Burma campaign. The 1st Provisional Tank Group had 1,800 personnel in six battalions, and was issued with between 100 and 125 M3A3 light tanks. On 19 April they were also given twelve M4A4 Shermans, which were organised into two platoons of six tanks each. (*Author's Collection*)

(**Opposite, above**) Kachin Rangers fire their Browning M1919 A4 heavy machine gun from their hilltop position towards Japanese lines. The Burmese irregulars were issued with the latest British and US weaponry, demonstrating their value to the Allied war effort. They also received uniforms, which often included US fatigue caps as worn by these two volunteers. One of their roles was to keep an eye on Japanese movements and to provide intelligence about them. (*Author's Collection*)

(**Opposite, below**) Three Kachin Rangers with a Bren gun and Lee Enfield rifles ready to fire from their ambush position against the Japanese in northern Burma. They were reported to have killed at least 3,000 Imperial Army troops during their operations behind enemy lines in Burma. In addition, they were said to have rescued 200 downed Allied airmen, blown up bridges and destroyed trains and other Japanese logistical targets. (*Author's Collection*)

(**Above**) A Kachin sharpshooter prepares to fire from the branch of a tree during operations by the irregular forces against the Japanese in March 1945. He had been issued with a basic uniform of shirt and shorts by the Allies, who gave a variety of clothing to their irregulars. The Kachins fought alongside the Chinese and US forces in northern Burma in 1943 and 1944, and were highly valued by the Allies for their jungle expertise. This man is armed with a Lee Enfield .303 rifle, issued to him by the British, and a lethal-looking traditional sword. (*Author's Collection*)

Lieutenant General Dan I. Sultan, commander of US and Chinese Nationalist Forces in Burma, is seen on a visit to the Mars Task Force in February 1945. He is travelling through the Newhkam Valley and had been given a mule to ride through the rough country in northern Burma. Sultan had taken command of the Mars Task Force in July 1944, along with a polyglot force of American, British, Chinese and Burmese natives. *(US National Archives)*

US Army doctor Major Strickland of the 335th Station Hospital along the Burma Road treats one of the thousands of Naga porters working for the Allies in January 1945. The tribes of Nagaland in the north-east border region of India and Burma were usually friendly to the Allied forces. Small numbers of Naga tribesmen did fight for the Japanese, but this was usually down to tribal rivalry. Major Strickland was one of the personnel of the all black staff at the 335th, in what the press of the time described as a 'Negro Hospital'. (*US National Archives*)

Chinese Nationalist heavy artillery is towed across a swollen stream during the advance on Lashio in March 1945. The retreating Japanese had destroyed the bridges across the numerous streams in the area, making life difficult for the advancing Chinese. The gun is a 155mm M1918, supplied by France to the USA and then handed over to their Chinese allies after 1942. (*Author's Collection*)

A junior officer of the Mars Task Force smiles for the camera as he moves up to the front carrying one of the newly issued M3 grease-gun sub-machine guns. The US Army began the war with the M1928 Thompson sub-machine gun but this was expensive to produce. M3s, which were issued in 1942, were a much cheaper option at $25 per gun, instead of $50 for a Thompson. (*US National Archives*)

(**Opposite, above**) The crew of a Mars Task Force M1A1 75mm PACK howitzer with a stack of shells ready to fire at Japanese positions. These shells had been transported through the difficult jungle terrain often on the backs of long-suffering mules. In the heat of the jungle the crew have all stripped to the waist in order to try to make serving their guns a little more bearable. (*US National Archives*)

(**Opposite, below**) A 40mm Bofors anti-aircraft gun belonging to the Mars Task Force on the look-out for any stray Japanese aircraft, although by 1944 Japanese aircraft were more of a nuisance than a major threat. By this date the Japanese Imperial Army and Navy air forces were totally outnumbered over Burma and usually operated in small units. These gunners look relaxed enough as they defend Myitkyina air strip, captured by the joint US-Chinese force a few months before. (*US National Archives*)

(**Above**) This probably contrived photograph features a US officer, a British commando and a Chinese Nationalist soldier. The 3rd Commando Brigade was sent to Burma and served mainly on the Arakan front in 1944–5, taking part in a number of landings along the coastline. It was made up of four commando regiments, two of Marine personnel and two of army personnel with a 'bayonet' strength of 540 men each. Reinforcements of elite troops like the Commandos had been promised by Winston Churchill in 1943 but did not arrive in numbers until 1944. One of the major operations undertaken by the brigade was the landing at Ramree Island, where it was supported by a troop of Sherman tanks, a battery of 25-pounders and a company of Indian Engineers. (*Author's Collection*)

(**Opposite, above**) Shan tribal volunteers from Detachment 101 line up for inspection before going on an operation in April 1945. The men are armed to the teeth with US-supplied weapons, including Thompson sub-machine guns. They also have Johnson M1941 automatic rifles, which were not in service with the regular US Army. One man has the Johnson light machine gun, which was based on the automatic rifle but was widely regarded as too delicate for jungle warfare. All the guerrillas wear a mix of Allied uniforms and have rather shabby US Army fatigue caps. (*Author's Collection*)

(**Opposite, below**) Chinese Nationalist soldiers in Burma wait patiently to be loaded onto the C-47 transport behind them to fly back to China. They belonged to the 22nd Division, which had served in Burma first in 1942 and then in 1944; having done their job, these troops were needed back home. Between 22 December 1944 and 5 January 1945 some 25,000 men, twenty-five 105mm field guns, forty-eight 75mm guns and a number of 4.2 mortars and 37mm anti-tank guns were also flown into China. (*US National Archives*)

Chinese Nationalist troops practise with their newly issued US bazookas in northern Burma in late July 1945. These soldiers had received US and British training either in India or western China and had then gone on to prove themselves in battle in 1944 and 1945. Their M1 launchers fired 2.36-in rockets that could penetrate up to 80mm of armour, with the thickest armour on a Japanese tank being 25mm. The vast majority of Chinese troops had been withdrawn across the China-Burma border to prepare for the coming civil war against the Communists. (*Author's Collection*)

Chapter Eleven

Crossing the Rivers
Autumn 1944–February 1945

On 3 July 1944 General Kawabe finally decided to end the disastrous Imphal operation, and what remained of the Japanese 15th Army now began a disorganised retreat from northern Burma. This terrible retreat was to see the deaths of thousands of Japanese and Indian troops of the INA. It was only the onset of the 1944 monsoon season that saved the 15th Army from complete destruction. General Slim had, however, already decided that the 14th Army was to continue operations during the monsoon. He was aware of the difficult conditions his men would face but knew that the Japanese would be suffering more. After crossing back into Burma, the Japanese retreat continued down the Kabaw Valley, moving south-eastwards towards the Chindwin river. Sent by Slim in pursuit of the 15th Army were 45,000 men of the 33rd Corps, out of its total strength of 88,500 men. In total, the 14th Army now had a ration strength of 260,000 men, while the Japanese force that they faced before reaching the Chindwin was 20,000 strong. This Japanese force consisted of four weak divisions and six independent brigades with little artillery and a handful of medium tanks. Despite their weaknesses, the Japanese turned on the pursuing 14th Army in a series of furious rearguard actions. The long pursuit continued from July to November. Although the British soldiers suffered in the conditions, they were in a much better state than their Japanese foes. Both armies often went hungry but the Japanese also had to contend with malnutrition and tropical diseases. By November the majority of the surviving 15th Army units had crossed the Chindwin river to relative safety. They had left behind most of their artillery and all of their tanks, and they were lucky if they had retained their rifles in the chaos. They had received a degree of air support from the Japanese Air Force, but by this stage in the campaign the Allies had 1,300 aircraft while the Japanese had only sixty-four.

The 66 year-old Japanese commander in central Burma, Lieutenant General H. Kimura, had decided to offer little resistance to the 14th Army's crossing of the Chindwin river. He would instead concentrate his forces along the line of the Irrawaddy river and attack the pursuing forces when they tried to cross. Kimura hastily reorganised his remaining forces. A New Burma Area Army was established, divided into three armies: the 33rd Army under 55-year-old Lieutenant General Masaka Honda, with two depleted divisions comprising 25,400 men, facing Sultan's Chinese-US Force; the 15th Army under Lieutenant General S. Katamura, with four divisions and 21,400 men, in central Burma around Mandalay; and the 28th Army under Lieutenant General S. Sakurai with three strong divisions in Arakan. Kimura's plan was to lure the 14th Army into central Burma, where he would defeat them as they crossed the Irrawaddy river. He hoped that the 14th would overextend its supply lines and would be susceptible to flank attacks by his troops. The only bright spot for the Japanese commander was the steady arrival of 30,000 reinforcements during the June–October period. Unfortunately, getting them from the south of Burma to his armies further north was difficult owing to the total lack of transport. He had requested 500 trucks, 2,000 pack animals and 45,000 tons of food, but received only a fraction of these vital supplies.

In order to advance into central Burma the 14th Army would have to cross two wide and fast-flowing rivers: the Chindwin and the Irrawaddy. The Chindwin ran north to south through northern Burma before joining the much longer and wider Irrawaddy, which ran for more than 1,000 miles through the country. The 14th Army spent the last months of 1944 advancing southwards down the west side of the Chindwin river. The first crossing of the Chindwin by the 33rd Corps took place at Sittaung on 4 December and was followed by crossings at Mawlaik and at Kalewa further south on the 24th. The units of the 33rd which had crossed the river were joined by a division coming down from the Indian base at Dimapur. The 33rd Corps forces now pushed eastwards towards Shwebo, while a division of the 4th Corps advanced in parallel and joined up with the 36th Division at Banbauk. Having established a number of bridgeheads, the majority of the 33rd Corps crossed the river and began to advance eastwards towards the next river obstacle, the Irrawaddy. It was expected that the Japanese would fortify the Zibyutaungdan mountain range 25 miles to the east of the Chindwin. When the 14th Army troops advanced to the mountains and outflanked them, they found that the Japanese had withdrawn most of their forces. It now became apparent that the Japanese did not want to fight the 14th Army on the flat country of the Shwebo Plain between the two rivers. This country naturally favoured the 14th Army's superiority in armour and the main Japanese opposition was expected once they crossed the Irrawaddy.

Two large 14th Army units, the 4th and 33rd Corps, were assigned to the Irrawaddy river crossings in early 1945. The 4th Corps consisted of the 7th and 17th Indian Divisions plus the 255th Tank Brigade equipped with Sherman tanks. It also had the four battalion-strong Lushai Brigade of Indian troops and the 28th East African Brigade. The 33rd Corps was composed of the 2nd, 19th and 20th Indian Divisions, the 254th Tank Brigade with Lee/Grant and Stuart tanks and the 268th Indian Motorised Brigade. The 19th Indian Division crossed the Irrawaddy at Thaneikkyin on

11 January and provoked a fierce Japanese counterattack – exactly the reaction Slim had hoped for. On 12 February there was another feigned crossing at Ngazun to the west of Mandalay. This also resulted in a Japanese counterattack, which further weakened Kimura's strength. These crossings were revealed as diversions two days later when the main assault took place 50 miles to the south-west at Pakokku. Once the 14th Army formations were across the river, they moved eastwards towards their objective at Meiktila. Once the 14th Army's divisions had crossed the Irrawaddy, the battle for central Burma could begin and both sides prepared for the decisive campaign.

Indian troops continue their advance down the Kabaw Valley in pursuit of the broken Japanese forces retreating from Imphal. General Slim's insistence on continuing to operate during the monsoon season was intended to give the Japanese no respite, dashing Japanese hopes for a lull in the fighting that would allow them to retire to new defensive lines to await the 14th Army's advance. (Author's Collection)

A column of mules from an Indian unit carrying their light machine guns along with their equipment and ammunition. The men are having to coax their long-suffering mules through a flooded field filled with the water from the monsoon of 1944. The old practice of halting most fighting during the monsoon was forgotten as the 14th Army moved in for the kill. The Indian troops came mostly from the north of the country, with some 189,000 serving in 1939. By 1945 there were 2.5 million Indian soldiers serving largely in the Far East, but the vast expansion of their numbers led to a dilution in the standard of these troops. (*Author's Collection*)

This Gurkha Bren gunner has just crossed a stream (or *chuang*), having rolled up his trousers and taken off his boots. There were dangers in crossing any water in Burma, with water leeches always waiting for any warm-blooded victim to attack. When a leech bit to suck blood from the victim they caused infections that were responsible for most jungle sores. Leeches also struck at sleeping soldiers, with one man finding more than a hundred bites on his body after a night in the open. (*Author's Collection*)

British soldiers relax during a break in the fighting in their jungle position in July 1944. Rest and relaxation were vitally important for British soldiers in the harsh environment of Burma. The small comforts that soldiers received helped to keep up their morale, as did a rum ration flown in when possible, although many British troops said they would have preferred beer to rum to quench their thirst, as well as cheer them up. (*Author's Collection*)

A British soldier moves through the undergrowth with his Thompson sub-machine gun to the fore in 1944. The old doctrine that the jungles of South-East Asia were impenetrable led to a lack of field training for British soldiers before 1941. There were some more enlightened officers in the 1930s who anticipated that the war in South-East Asia would not be fought strictly along roads. Manuals on jungle warfare were issued in 1940 in Malaya but this did not prevent the defeat of the Allies there in 1942. After 1942 jungle training for the British and Indian Army was vastly improved but not all the lessons had been learned by the time of the first Arakan offensive in 1942–3. (*Cody Images*)

An officer of the 5th Indian Division makes a reconnaissance of the Japanese positions along the Tiddim-Kalewa Road in October 1944. The men are looking towards the enemy mountain stronghold established on the 8,800ft high Kennedy Peak. Once this Japanese position, just to the north of the Chindwin river had been taken, the town of Kalewa fell on 14 November. This officer has not removed the pips on his shoulder boards, which could have given away his rank to any alert Japanese snipers. Snipers were trained to pick off any officers, and rank insignia and the different uniforms worn by British and Indian Army higher ranks were a gift to them. *(Author's Collection)*

A Gurhka poses proudly for the cameraman in the vicinity of Kennedy Peak, which was held by the 5th Indian Division. Gurkhas earned a fine reputation for their fighting abilities and sheer fearlessness, but were also said to have their weaknesses. Wingate criticised them for being too noisy in the jungle and giving their positions away. The Gurkhas had little respect for Wingate, remarking that his jungle experience was poor and that he had seen service only in the deserts of Palestine in the 1930s and Ethiopia in 1941. During the Burma campaign the 6th and 7th Gurkha Rifles served along with the 4/1st, 4/4th , 4/5th and 4/8th Battalions. *(Author's Collection)*

Men of the 7th Indian Division advancing towards Fort White near Tiddim, which fell to them on 7 December 1944. A combined force from the 7th and 17th Divisions took the Japanese stronghold to the south of Imphal as they pursued the retreating Imperial Army. Their objective was to reach Pakokku to the south-west of Mandalay to cut off the Japanese 15th Army. (*Author's Collection*)

The capture of the town of Kalewa by the 11th East African Division in early December 1944 allowed the building of a Bailey bridge across the Chindwin river. Its construction was a major endeavour by the Royal Engineers, largely due to the conditions in which it was built. At the time this bridge was photographed it was still under construction, but when finished it was the longest Bailey bridge ever built, at 365yds. (*Cody Images*)

(**Opposite, above**) A flotilla of DUKW amphibious vehicles packed full of supplies moves down the Chindwin river. Burma's river system was used to move supplies from unit to unit, but the lack of suitable craft meant that this transport method was limited. Priority for these amphibious vehicles was given to the European campaigns in France and Italy in 1944 and early 1945. When Nazi Germany was defeated in May 1945, some of these valuable vehicles were released for use in the Far East. (*Author's Collection*)

(**Opposite, below**) British troops cross the Irrawaddy river at Tigyiang with a supply raft improvised from three boats with outboard engines lashed together with a wooden platform added. The shortage of boats and landing craft meant that a great deal of ingenuity had to be employed at times to get across the rivers of lower Burma. The Irrawaddy river was up to a mile wide near Mandalay, causing great problems for the 14th Army. (*US National Archives*)

(**Above**) A Gurkha unit of the 36th Division heading for Katha crosses the Irrawaddy in an assault boat with their mules lashed to the side. These mules have their heads kept above the water but inevitably there were some that broke loose and drowned. One of the largest rivers in Asia, the Irrawaddy had to be crossed using a motley armada of assault craft, rafts and civilian wooden boats. As was usual for the 14th Army, its soldiers had to improvise due to the shortage of hardware compared to the Allied forces in Europe and the Pacific. (*Author's Collection*)

(**Opposite, above**) A DUKW amphibious carrier comes ashore on the eastern bank of the Irrawaddy after an unopposed crossing. These purpose-built landing craft were in desperately short supply until some of the thousands used in Normandy in 1944 could be transported to the Far East. There were only nine DUKWs per division in Burma, which was totally inadequate for the tasks they were asked to perform. (*Author's Collection*)

(**Opposite, below**) A Gurkha of the 4th Battalion, 4th Gurkha Rifles, 19th Indian Division, fires from cover with his Sten Mk 3 sub-machine gun. The 19th Division made a rapid march from the town of Indaw and crossed the Irrawaddy at Thabeijkkyin on 19 January. Having established a secure bridgehead on the other side the division faced heavy Japanese counterattacks. The Japanese saw the crossing on the 19th as a threat to Mandalay and expected more crossings at various points along the river. (*Author's Collection*)

(**Above**) Soldiers of the 9th Battalion, Borders Regiment, move cautiously through a village during a mopping-up operation against remnants of the Japanese army. The majority of the regiment's recruits came from the north-western border counties of Cumberland and Westmoreland. Other recruits came from County Durham, giving the whole regiment a strictly northern flavour. (*Cody Images*)

River landing craft speed along a river with two of the rear boat's crew keeping a close watch on the bank. Even in areas that had been liberated by Allied forces there was still a danger from Japanese troops. As the 14th Army advanced, a number of smaller formations of Imperial Army soldiers were bypassed. Many of these Japanese hold-outs still had to be dealt with and the rivers of Burma were used to send units out to subdue them. (*Cody Images*)

Two British soldiers fire from cover, having landed with their unit on the eastern bank of the Irrawaddy river in February 1945. The Japanese had withdrawn units from the 28th Army in Arakan and from other sectors to defend the Irrawaddy and Chindwin rivers. Two main bridgeheads were established across the Irrawaddy, at Ngazun on 13 February and at Nyuangu a day later. Although the Japanese troops tried to defend their defensive lines, there were too few of them to prevent the Allied crossings. (*Author's Collection*)

Chapter Twelve

The Fall of Meiktila and Mandalay February–March 1945

General Slim knew that the Japanese forces remaining in central and southern Burma were still substantial in early 1945. Despite the 14th Army's superiority in heavy weapons and the Allied air force's total air superiority, which meant that final victory was virtually assured, Slim also knew that the fighting would be hard, regardless of the advantages his forces now held. His plan for the coming fighting in central Burma in 1945 was a strategic masterstroke. The 14th Army's two main objectives in central Burma were the city of Mandalay and the town of Meiktila, some 80 miles distant. Meiktila, an important rail and road intersection, was the main supply hub for the Japanese Army. The Japanese commanders expected the 14th Army's first attacks to fall on the city of Mandalay, but Slim had decided to attack Meiktila for its strategic value. He fully intended to use his total superiority in tanks and artillery to full advantage against the Japanese. The flat country in central Burma was also ideal for his armoured columns to crush Japanese resistance with their handful of anti-tank guns.

General Slim's plan was for the majority of the 14th Army to continue its advance towards the Irrawaddy. Meanwhile most of his 4th Corps was to cross the river at Nyaungu under radio silence in preparation to outflank the Japanese defences. The 33rd Corps was to advance to the Irrawaddy, cross the river and then make a frontal attack against Mandalay. As the Japanese advanced to destroy the 33rd Corps' bridge-heads over the Irrawaddy, the 4th Corps would advance to attack Meiktila, forcing the Japanese to withdraw troops from the defence of Mandalay to assist the defenders at Meiktila. With the defences of Mandalay diminished, the garrisons of the two objectives of the 14th Army's offensive could be destroyed piecemeal. The 19th Indian Division crossed the Irrawaddy river to the north of Mandalay between 7 and 11 January and established fortified bridgeheads; as expected, the Japanese launched a series of desperate attacks to dislodge them. On 12 February the 20th Indian Division crossed the Irrawaddy to the south of Mandalay and dug in, waiting for the Japanese response. As expected, the two-pronged attack forced the Japanese to divide their forces. General Kimura was soon to receive a further shock. On 14 February the 7th Indian Division crossed the river at Nyaungu against a weakened defence force. To the south of Mandalay the 2nd British Division crossed the Irrawaddy on the 24th, further confusing the Japanese as to where the next attack was coming from.

The 19th Indian Division now began its advance on Mandalay, which was defended by a 3,500-strong garrison. In the meantime the 17th Indian Division, now reinforced by the 255th Armoured Brigade, moved towards Meiktila. On the 27 February these forces surrounded the town and began their assault. The town was defended by 3,200 Japanese, many of whom were service and second-line troops. The defenders also included 400 patients who had been pushed out of the town's military hospitals and armed with bamboo spears! The Allied tanks faced just a handful of anti-tank guns. The town's defences were largely reliant on booby traps, and soldiers waiting in trenches to throw themselves at tanks carrying primed artillery shells. After heavy fighting Meiktila was finally taken on 3 March, with the Japanese suffering 2,000 losses. Once in Allied hands, the town came under the expected heavy frontal counter-attacks from the Japanese. While these attacks were taking place, the remainder of the 33rd Corps was advancing to trap any Japanese units left around Meiktila. The Allied garrison was supplied by air, and its tanks were employed in 'active' defence destroying Japanese strongholds. Kimura was obsessed with retaking Meiktila, although the town's importance would be ended if the city of Mandalay fell.

The battle for Mandalay had been going on at the same time as the fighting at Meiktila, and the city had been heavily fortified by the Japanese. They turned temples and other buildings into fortresses and had to be winkled out by the 14th Army's heavy artillery and by air strikes. Mandalay finally fell on the 20/21 March after house-to-house fighting, and attention turned to the continuing battle for Meiktila. Now the combined 33rd and 4th Corps could concentrate on destroying the remaining Japanese around Meiktila. By 22 March these forces were in touch with the Meiktila garrison, and they were united by the 24th. Sufficient Allied formations had arrived at Meiktila by the 29th to overwhelm the already devastated Japanese. The remaining Japanese in central Burma were ordered to withdraw southwards. Their commander, General Kimura, used the Mandalay-Thazi railway to escape with a large number of his troops. The Japanese had been crushed between the rapidly moving units of the 14th Army just as Slim had planned. All of central Burma was now in Allied hands, and they were now moving to take their next major objective, the capital Rangoon. The fall of Meiktila and Mandalay was effectively the end for the Japanese in central Burma and their losses were devastating. Casualties were probably underestimated at 28,700, with 617 captured during the fighting. Materially the losses were equally devastating, with 430 precious artillery pieces captured and all tanks destroyed. British losses were also heavy, with 13,000 casualties including 2,800 dead, and thirty of their tanks destroyed, although no artillery pieces were lost.

Soldiers of the East Lancashire Regiment cross one of the thousands of *chuangs* or streams that lay in the path of the Allied advance. Once these men had crossed the *chuang*, they would have to carry their rubber assault boat to the next stream. Although this type of craft was relatively light, the collapsible boats were much heavier and might have to be carried for miles to the next *chuang*. In any conditions this kind of labour would have been tiring but in the humid conditions of Burma it was almost unbearable. (*Author's Collection*)

(**Above**) A mortar unit of the 19th Indian Division fire from their jungle position towards the Japanese during the advance on Mandalay. Their Mk IV 3-in mortars were the main type used by the British and Indian troops during the Burma campaign. Some were improved by increasing the strength of the mortar's baseplate, which gave them a range of 2,750yd. A new, lighter Mk V version was produced before the end of the war but only 5,000 had been manufactured by then. (*Cody Images*)

(**Opposite, above**) RAF flight mechanics at work on their squadron's Thunderbolt P-47 fighters, which were flying from a forward airstrip in March 1945. The US-built Thunderbolts took part in ground attacks against railways, docks, airstrips and other Japanese assets, using their wing-mounted cannon. They were more than able to deal with any Japanese fighters that tried to interfere with their attack missions. (*Author's Collection*)

(**Opposite, below**) A trio of British soldiers in their trench waiting to deal with any Japanese counterattacks in early 1945. They are equipped with all the main weapons used by the British Army in the fighting in Burma in 1943–5. Sten sub-machine guns, Lee Enfield rifles and Bren machine guns were the mainstays of the British and Indian Armies. (*Cody Images*)

(**Opposite, above**) The crew of an M3A1 Honey light tank prepare their vehicle to move off during the fighting in early 1945. They are removing the camouflage covers from the tank, although by this stage in the campaign there were few Japanese planes to worry about. This tank belonged to the 7th Light Cavalry of the Indian Armoured Corps, which played a major role in the defeat of the Japanese in 1944–5. (*Author's Collection*)

(**Opposite, below**) A dead Japanese soldier crouches with a 250lb aerial bomb still between his knees. Like hundreds of other volunteers, he had been given the task of ambushing the oncoming Allied tanks outside Meiktila. Known as the Nikwhaku Kogeki – 'Human Combat Destruction Squad' – they were totally fixated with their deadly mission. They were so fixated that British troops often quietly approached them from the flanks and shot them at close range. The British dismissed these suicide troops by calling them, in the dark humour of war, 'Toads in the Hole'. (*Author's Collection*)

(**Above**) A Priest M8 self-propelled gun moves at speed along a dusty road during the offensive to take Meiktila. The Priest mounted a 105mm howitzer on the chassis of a Sherman medium tank and gave the Allies a potent weapon not available to the Japanese. Although there were self-propelled guns in the Imperial Army, they were built in such small numbers that they were irrelevant. (*Janusz Piekalkiewicz Collection*)

(**Opposite, above**) The crew of a Priest M8 self-propelled gun rush to man their vehicle as an alarm sounds. These US-supplied armoured vehicles gave the crews some degree of protection from enemy fire while they manned their main armament. One of the crew mans the Browning M2 heavy machine gun in case of attacks from Japanese infantry. (*Cody Images*)

(**Opposite, below**) Indian National Army volunteers hand over their ex-British Lee Enfield rifles with fixed bayonets to their British captors at Mount Popa to the west of Meiktila in March 1945. Most of the men also wear ex-British khaki drill uniforms, which were captured in large numbers at the fall of Singapore in 1942. How useful the INA was to the Japanese in Burma is open to debate, but many did fight well and thousands died in their quest for Indian independence. (*Author's Collection*)

(**Above**) Soldiers of the 2nd 'Dagger' Division move cautiously through the debris of a firefight on the western approaches to Mandalay in mid-March 1945. The advance along the southern banks of the Irrawaddy river drove a wedge between the two main Japanese forces. In the foreground lie the bodies of Japanese troops killed in the fighting a few minutes before. Soldiers always had to be wary of the possibility that presumed dead Japanese troops were simply playing dead and waiting for the opportunity to attack them as they moved past. (*Author's Collection*)

A sergeant of the Lushai Brigade pictured in February 1945 during the advance to Mandalay. The Lushai Brigade, made up of various Burmese ethnic groups, was commanded by the 'swashbuckling' Brigadier P.C. Marindin. It operated in the hills between Manipur and Arakan at the start of the fighting in 1943. During the fighting in central Burma in early 1945 the brigade's irregulars were employed in blocking Japanese escape routes. They showed no mercy to Japanese troops that fell into their hands, and were reported to have inflicted heavy casualties on them. (*Author's Collection*)

(**Opposite, above**) At least a dozen artillerymen manhandle a QF 25-pounder Mk 2 field gun up a slope to help the truck that is struggling to pull it. This medium gun was designed in 1936 but did not see service until the Norwegian campaign of 1940. It was developed to meet a new required range of 13,700ft specified by the Royal Artillery. About 12,000 were produced and they served on every front in the Second World War; some examples were still in use with some units in the early 1970s. (*Author's Collection*)

(**Opposite, below**) Soldiers of the 14th Army move across open ground on the approaches to the town of Meiktila. The town, which was 80 miles south of Mandalay, was the main centre of land communications in Burma. Meiktila was cleared of the Japanese on 3 March and the British continued to advance towards their next target, the capital of Burma: Rangoon. (*Author's Collection*)

(**Above**) Vehicles of the 62nd Motorised Brigade move along the road from the Nyuangu bridgehead and Meiktila. The Japanese tried to defend as many crossing points over the Irrawaddy as possible but their forces were too thinly spread. Vehicles in this column include Sherman M4 medium tanks, Universal carriers with canopies added, light trucks and motorcycles. Fast-moving columns like this could sweep aside the poorly armed Japanese forces sent to try to stop their progress. *(Janusz Piekalkiewicz Collection)*

(**Opposite**) A Sherman M4 medium tank of the Indian Army's Probyn's Horse Regiment moves forward during the battle for central Burma. The arrival of better tanks in Burma from 1944 was largely down to General Frank Messervy, who had been Director of Armoured Vehicles before taking command of the 7th Indian Division. He demanded that tanks heavier than the M3A1 Honeys should be sent as soon as possible to Burma. Some officers in the Indian armoured formations still thought that light tanks were the best that could operate in the Burmese jungle, but Messervy argued that Shermans would be impervious to Japanese anti-tank guns, whereas Honeys could be disabled by them. *(Author's Collection)*

(**Above**) Soldiers of the 6/7th Rajput Rifles hitch a ride on a Sherman M4 medium tank belonging to the famous Probyn's Horse Regiment. They had been taking part in a search for Japanese stragglers in the jungle around Meiktila. The rapid advance of the Allied armoured forces meant that some Japanese defences were bypassed and had to be dealt with later. (*Janusz Piekalkiewicz Collection*)

(**Opposite, above**) This Japanese press photograph purports to show Imperial Army light artillery during the battle for Mandalay. They are firing a Type 92 70mm battalion gun, which was one of the mainstays of the Japanese light artillery from 1932 until 1945. This lightweight gun could easily be manhandled by its crew, and had another advantage in that its barrel could be traversed up to 90 degrees. In a jungle environment the high traverse meant that shells could be fired down on the enemy at relatively close range. Another advantage was that it could be moved from firing position to firing position in a relatively short time. (*Author's Collection*)

(**Opposite, below**) A patrol of Indian troops use the wall of a bombed building for cover on the outskirts of Mandalay in March 1945. The Sikh soldier in the centre is wearing a light khaki or jungle green turban supplied by the Indian Army. His two comrades are wearing a new style of jungle green cap with built-in neck flap to protect the wearer from the sun. By this stage of the war the old khaki drill uniforms had been largely replaced by jungle green ones. (*Author's Collection*)

(**Opposite, above**) British troops move past the body of a dead Japanese soldier who broke from cover to attack them during their advance on Mandalay. Right up the end of the Burma campaign few Japanese were willing to be taken prisoner, and Allied troops were loath to take them alive. British and Indian soldiers' attitudes to the Japanese had been hardened by witnessing the horrific treatment meted out to their captured comrades. (*Author's Collection*)

(**Opposite, below**) Two Indian soldiers fire from a deserted building on the outskirts of Mandalay in March 1945. The machine-gunner has two large tropical water bottles slung over his shoulder, and both men have British Army-issue machetes. Gas masks were carried by some soldiers as the Japanese Army throughout the world was known to use chemical weapons. (*Cody Images*)

(**Above**) The crew of a 5.5-in field gun fire at close range into Japanese defensive positions in the historic Fort Dufferin at Mandalay. This old fortress had walls that were 30ft high and 12ft thick, and it was surrounded by a moat 70yd wide. The Japanese defenders fought fanatically to hold the fort before its walls were destroyed on 19 March 1945. It was not British artillery that finally breached the walls but bombs dropped by Mitchell B-25 bombers. (*Janusz Piekalkiewicz Collection*)

(**Opposite, above**) A squad of British troops moving from cover to cover as they capture the village of Ywathitgyi on the road to Mandalay. The village was bitterly defended by a few Japanese troops who refused to surrender this unimportant hamlet. During the fighting in central Burma small engagements like this were costly to both sides, with the Japanese in most cases fighting to the last man. (*Author's Collection*)

(**Opposite, below**) A Sherman M4 tank and accompanying infantry move towards a pagoda in the suburbs of Mandalay, which the Japanese have turned into yet another stronghold, on 10 March. Thousands of Allied troops were employed in mopping up any last vestiges of resistance from the Japanese. Although the morale of the Imperial Army had been affected by their defeats in Burma, there were still many who were prepared to fight to the death for the Emperor. (*Janusz Piekalkiewicz Collection*)

(**Above**) Sikh soldiers who took part in the capture of the Burmese oilfields north of Chauk were left in their foxholes to guard a number of oil storage tanks. Large numbers of Japanese troops were caught between the city of Meiktila and the Yenangyuang oil fields. They were in a poor condition after the fighting for Meiktila and were more interested in breaking out towards the Sittang river than in fighting the advancing Allied troops. (*Author's Collection*)

This Type 88 75mm Japanese anti-aircraft gun was captured at Yenangyuang, where the oilfields so coveted by the Imperial Army in 1942 were centred. The oilfields fell to the rapidly advancing 7th Indian Division on 22 April before the Japanese could organise a defence. General Slim was both surprised and exultant at the swift capture of the oilfields, as he expected much stronger resistance from the Japanese. (*Author's Collection*)

In the aftermath of the liberation of Mandalay, a young couple venture back into their village which has been cleared of Japanese troops. They lived in the village of Sadaung, 35 miles north-west of the city, and had fled from there when the fighting began. For transport they have a Burmese rickshaw, which looks like a bicycle and motorcycle sidecar combination. There was little enthusiasm among the Burmese population for either side and, as one commentator said, there were no flag-waving crowds to greet the victorious Allied troops. (*Author's Collection*)

An alleyway in the centre of Mandalay full of rotting corpses of Japanese soldiers killed a few days before in the intense fighting for the city. By this stage in the war most Imperial Army soldiers knew that they were going to be defeated by the Allies. Despite their impending defeat, many Japanese were still prepared to die fighting for their Emperor. (*Author's Collection*)

Chapter Thirteen

The Road to Rangoon

After the fall of central Burma and the cities of Mandalay and Meiktila in March 1945, the next objective for the 14th Army's offensive was the important port and capital of Burma, Rangoon. There was a debate in the Allied command as to the best way to capture it. As early as 1942 there had been proposals to land Allied forces on the southern coast of Burma to liberate the city, but any amphibious operation would require the use of the ports on the Arakan coast, which were still held by the Japanese. In January 1945 the 14th Army began operations to capture these ports, from which a seaborne attack on Rangoon could be launched. This was planned to coincide with the landward advance against Rangoon which would follow the 14th Army's taking of central Burma. On 4 January units of the 14th Army took Akyab Island off the Arakan coast in an unopposed amphibious landing. A few weeks later on the 21st the 71st Brigade of the 26th Indian Division landed further down the coast on Ramree Island. The 26th Division then spent February clearing the Japanese out of Arakan and then underwent amphibious warfare training in preparation for the attack on Rangoon. This training was to continue for a few months, during which time the 26th Division was kept out of the front lines ready to strike in late April. On 22 February another amphibious landing took place at Kangow in the Bay of Bengal. These successful landings would now permit an amphibious operation to take Rangoon from the sea when the time was right.

Despite their heavy defeats at both Meiktila and Mandalay, the Japanese were not yet ready to give up on their control of southern Burma. They hoped to stop the 14th Army's advance on Rangoon, which was to involve a two-pronged advance by the 4th and 33rd Corps. Facing the 14th Army advance was the Japanese 28th Army, which had been sent from Arakan to support the defence of central Burma. It had arrived too late to influence the situation there but was now available to fight the 14th Army. Compared to other Japanese formations in southern Burma, the 28th was more or less intact, having suffered fewer casualties in its Arakan campaign. Also available to defend the other route to Rangoon from Meiktila through Toungoo were the remnants of the heavily defeated 33rd and 15th Japanese Armies. On 11 April the 300-mile advance on Rangoon began with the 4th Corps moving down the Sittang

Valley. At the same time the 33rd Corps moved down the main road to the south leading to the city of Prome. The 14th Army's mobile columns of tanks and other armoured vehicles moved quickly, sweeping aside the Japanese who were often surprised by the speed of their advance. By 14 April the 5th Indian Division was at Yamathan, 40 miles south-east of Meiktila. Four days later the 5th had captured the city of Shwemyo, without meeting any major Japanese resistance. They were then held to the south of the city by stiffening Japanese defence. On 20 April the 4th Corps entered Toungoo and nine days later they had reached Kadok, 70 miles from Rangoon. To the west of the main offensive the 4th Corps' 7th Indian Division captured Kyaukpadang on 12 April. On the 21st they surrounded the city of Yenangyuang and the oilfields that surrounded it. While the 33rd Corps was pushing southwards towards Rangoon, much of the 4th Corps became bogged down in mopping-up Japanese resistance around Yenangyuang. On 22 April the 5th Indian Division, 4th Corps, took the important Japanese airfield at Toungoo, having advanced 50 miles in three days. On the same day the Japanese commander General Kimura ordered the withdrawal of the bulk of his troops from Rangoon. They were told to head for the shelter of the Pegu Yomas mountains in preparation for a move to the south-eastern border region. Kimura chose to refuse an order from Field Marshal Hisaichi Terauchi, commander-in-chief of the Southern Area Army, to try to hold Rangoon. According to Kimura, Terauchi was out of touch with the situation on the ground. His carefully worded refusal said: 'I admired the sentiment expressed in the message, but I was at the same time astounded by the complete ignorance of the actual situation shown by the staff of Southern Army.' By 29 April the 20th Indian Division, 33rd Corps, had captured Allanmyo on the Irrawaddy river less than 40 miles from Prome.

With Arakan fully secured by the 15th Corps, by 28 April the forces there were ready to launch a seaborne attack on Rangoon. On 30 April began the long-planned amphibious attack on Rangoon, codenamed Operation Dracula, with the 26th Indian Division, 15th Corps, sailing from the Arakan coast. The assault on Rangoon now involved amphibious, parachute and land forces in a well coordinated attack. On 1 May two Gurkha parachute battalions landed at the mouth of the Irrawaddy river to the south of the city. The following day the 26th Indian Division launched its amphibious force from the Arakan ports. The invasion armada sailed along the coast through the eastern region of the Bay of Bengal towards Rangoon, arriving south of the city on 3 May. The troops disembarked and were soon ready to move towards Rangoon; they were able to advance into an almost totally deserted city. Units of the 26th met up with the vanguard of the 17th Indian Division at Hlegu, moving from the north into Rangoon on 6 May. In the immediate aftermath of Rangoon's fall there were the usual mopping-up operations, taking care of any remaining Japanese forces. Despite the defeat of the Japanese around Rangoon, there were still substantial numbers of troops of the 28th Army at large in southern Burma. As the various 14th Army forces converged on Rangoon, they effectively cut off the majority of the 28th Army from the remaining Japanese forces in southern Burma. On 26 May the 33rd Corps occupied Bassein, an important railway town approximately 80 miles to the west of Rangoon. The 14th Army's objectives were now to concentrate on destroying the remaining Japanese forces at large in south-east Burma.

General C.E.N. Lomax, commander of the 26th Indian Division (*left*), chatting with Lieutenant General Philip Christison, commander of the 15th Corps. General Christison was given command of the Arakan operation planned to take place in early 1945, and had under his command the 81st and 82nd West African Divisions and the 25th Indian Division. In addition, he had the 3rd Commando Brigade, a squadron of medium tanks and an artillery regiment. His corps also had air support from 200 aircraft and naval support from three Royal Navy cruisers. (*Author's Collection*)

A Gurkha fires his Thompson sub-machine gun towards Japanese lines on 12 January 1945 during the landings at Kangaw on the Arakan coast. Kangaw, a town on the Myebon Peninsula, was fought over for over a week. The heaviest fighting centred on Hill 170, which dominated the town. It was attacked by a unit of No. 1 Commando and after it was captured they had to deal with a week of Japanese counterattacks. (*Author's Collection*)

(**Opposite, above**) Early 1945 saw the Allied conquest of the islands off the southern coast of Arakan, with landings taking place on the main island of Ramree on 21 January. Some 50 miles long by 20 miles wide, Ramree Island saw heavy fighting, with the Japanese garrison being totally destroyed by early March. Here Indian troops land on the beach before moving inland to tackle the dug-in Japanese defenders. (*Author's Collection*)

(**Opposite, below**) Engineers gathering Japanese sea mines on a landing beach on the Myebon Peninsula in January 1945. They had landed on the peninsula, 35 miles from the Arakanese port of Akyab, on the 12th. Sea mines accounted for a number of Allied landing craft and ships during amphibious operations in 1945. During the landings on the Arakan coast they lost one landing craft support (LCS), two landing craft personnel (LCPs) and four landing craft mechanised (LCMs). (*Author's Collection*)

(**Above**) Two B-29 Super Fortresses of the 486th Bombardment Group of XX Bomber Command are seen over Rangoon in February 1945. The raids by these huge bombers devastated large parts of the Burmese capital, with the port facilities a main target. Super Fortresses operated from bases in northern India close to the western end of the Ledo Road. (*Author's Collection*)

(**Opposite, above**) Indian soldiers of the Frontier Force Rifles, 15th Indian Corps, launch an attack on a steep hill on the approaches to the town of Taungue in Arakan on 13 March 1945. The landing on the Arakan coastline was covered by a special decoy unit known as D-Force. The last Japanese supply base, this town was captured on 13 April 1945. By this date the vast majority of Japanese troops had withdrawn from Arakan and taken up new defensive positions further east. (*Author's Collection*)

(**Opposite, below**) Volunteers of the Burmese National Army march out of their barracks under the command of a Japanese officer. On 28 March 1945 the 11,000-strong BNA moved out of its bases in Rangoon to fight the 'hated' British. Unknown to the Japanese, the BNA commander Aung San had made a deal with the Allies and his force turned on their former sponsors, killing large numbers of Imperial Army advisers and men. (*Author's Collection*)

This photograph featuring the tank commander of a Type 97 tankette was captured by Allied troops in 1945. It was found on the dead body of the light tank's driver during the fighting in Arakan in March that year. The Type 97 was a totally outgunned armoured vehicle with only 12mm of armour plating and a 37mm main armament. Not only were Japanese tanks outclassed, by 1945 they were also heavily outnumbered. (*RHQ DWR via George Forty*)

A supply column of light trucks belonging to the 17th Indian Division move through a village on the outskirts of Rangoon in April 1945. The 17th had been formed in 1941 and had served in Malaya and then in the retreat from Burma in 1942. As in most modern campaigns, the majority of soldiers were involved in logistics and other second-line roles. By this point in the war the rear areas of the Allied forces were much safer than they had been previously as the Japanese did not have the forces to ambush columns like this. (*Author's Collection*)

Paratroopers of the Indian Army in training during the build-up to their most important operation of the Burma campaign. On 1 May 1945 the Gurkha Parachute Battalion was dropped onto Elephant Point, which controlled the entrance to Rangoon harbour. The Indian Army had had a parachute formation since October 1942, with separate Indian and Gurkha battalions formed into a brigade. Its first actions saw it fighting on the Burma-Indian border in an heroic action which cost it a staggering 580 casualties. (*Author's Collection*)

(**Opposite, above**) Reinforcements are landed by LCLs at Elephant Point near Rangoon, which had been captured the day before by Indian paratroopers. The soldiers are walking gingerly along the path at the side of a paddy field, as none of them wants to get a soaking. One of the main problems for the 14th Army was the shortage of landing craft and other small boats needed for amphibious warfare. (*Cody Images*)

(**Opposite, below**) Royal Navy landing craft and ships approach Rangoon with the burning port facilities in the background. Most of the Japanese troops in Rangoon had marched to meet the main Allied advance coming from the north. They fought to the north of Rangoon at Pegu and the Imperial Army units were heavily defeated, with few Japanese left to fight for the capital. (*Author's Collection*)

(**Above**) While the fighting went on across Burma, the Allies' navies were regaining control of the Indian Ocean. The Allied East Indies Fleet had sunk a large number of Japanese merchant ships in the 1943–5 period. By the end of the war the Japanese were relying on a polyglot fleet of unsuitable vessels to try to keep the Imperial Army in Burma supplied. These ferry-boats, coasters, junks and sampans crept down the coastline of China before heading through the Malacca Straits. Waiting for them were a number of Royal Navy and US submarines, along with surface ships, which sank the majority of them. These two Royal Navy officers are searching for any Japanese vessels which managed to get close to Burma. (*Author's Collection*)

(**Above**) During the fighting for Toungoo in April 1945 curious Gurkhas peer past a dead Japanese soldier who was shot as he emerged from this dug-out. The Japanese were experts at constructing jungle fortifications during the Burma campaign. Because building materials were in very short supply, the Japanese had to build their dug-outs with tree trunks. These wooden superstructures gave little protection from mortar or artillery fire. They would camouflage their strongpoints and wait for Allied troops to approach before opening fire. (*Author's Collection*)

(**Opposite, above**) Symbolic of the cooperation between the British, US and Chinese forces in Burma in 1944–5, an American doctor treats an injured Gurkha. The doctor, who was reported by the journalist to be from New York, belonged to the American Field Service. While he patches up their comrade, other Gurkhas look out for any counterattack by the embattled Japanese. (*Author's Collection*)

(**Opposite, below**) A mountain battery of the Indian artillery was carried to the front on the backs of the unit's mules during the advance into southern Burma. During the 1945 monsoon moving guns like this into position while knee-deep in mud was, to say the least, difficult. This 3.7-in pack howitzer, a type that was first issued in 1917, was operating in support of the Allied advance on the Burmese city of Toungoo. (*Author's Collection*)

(**Opposite, above**) An Indian Army 3.7-in pack howitzer fires towards Japanese positions in the foothills of southern Burma. The type had been used mainly by the Indian Army before 1939 in fighting the various rebellions on the north-west frontier of India. Although rather archaic looking, the gun was to provide valuable support for the British forces in the fighting of 1944–5. (*Author's Collection*)

(**Opposite, below**) A column of light armoured vehicles and jeeps passing smartly dressed Gurkhas on the road to Rangoon. At the same time as the main motorised force was moving southwards towards the Burmese capital, other forces were also moving on the city. There was an amphibious landing by the 26th Division in the Gulf of Martaban to the south of Rangoon, while the 17th Indian Division took Pegu, 40 miles from Rangoon, on 2 May. On the same day an air landing by the Gurkha Parachute Battalion to the south of the city squeezed the vice on the Japanese garrison. (*Author's Collection*)

(**Above**) Soldiers of the East Yorkshire Regiment marching from the north into Rangoon as the city fell to the 14th Army. The heavy kit carried by these troops must have been difficult to bear in the heat of Burma. Some of the men are carrying more than one weapon and one has two water canteens. Perhaps the trucks in the background were going to take the men's heavier equipment into the city for them. During night marches British soldiers were often issued with tags dipped in phosphorus paint which they fastened to the back of their pack so that the man behind could easily follow. (*Author's Collection*)

Two flame-thrower operators of the 14th Army blast a Japanese bunker on the approaches to Rangoon. They are both equipped with the Flamethrower Portable No. 2 Mk 2, nicknamed 'Lifebuoy', which was the main type in service with the British Army. Each carries on his back the doughnut-shaped fuel tank containing 4 gallons of fuel, which when ignited could shoot flames up to 110ft. Because of the Japanese reluctance to surrender for most of the Burma campaign this weapon was often called in. When the Japanese were too well dug-in for a costly infantry assault, the flamethrowers usually solved the problem. *(Author's Collection)*

Soldiers of a Punjab regiment march out of the jungle after a strenuous patrol 15 miles west of Pyagle on the Mandalay-Rangoon road. Indian troops were the backbone of the Allied war effort in Burma and their bravery in action meant they received many awards. Twenty Victoria Crosses were awarded during the Burma campaign, fourteen of them to Indian/Gurkha soldiers.

(Author's Collection)

A British soldier frogmarches a captured Japanese sniper, stripped of his uniform, through the town of Pegu, north of Rangoon. Pegu was captured on 29 April by the 17th Indian Division commanded by General Cowan. For Cowan it was a bittersweet moment as his troops had passed through the same town during the desperate 1942 retreat. (*Author's Collection*)

A British patrol moves in single file at pace across flooded open country during the advance southwards by the 14th Army. In the open like this they were in danger of coming under fire from any remaining Japanese positions and stay-behind snipers. Isolated units of Japanese troops who were still willing to die for the emperor built strongpoints in a number of villages and hamlets. When available, Allied fighters and fighter-bombers would be called in to strike at the Japanese defenders before the infantry went in to clear the remnants. (*Author's Collection*)

Major General F.W. Festing (*left*), commander of the 36th Division, and to his right Major General D.J. 'Punch' Cowan, commander of the 17th Indian Division, photographed on the approach to Rangoon watching a motorised column of their troops heading for the Burmese capital in the last days before its fall. General Festing had had a frank discussion with General Stilwell when his division was joined by the US-Chinese force in northern China. He had gained Stilwell's grudging respect by speaking to him in the same honest manner that Stilwell himself used.

(*Author's Collection*)

(**Opposite, above**) Soldiers of the RAF Regiment land from a landing craft on the coast close to Rangoon as the Burmese capital falls to the 14th Army. The ground troops of the regiment were responsible for guarding air bases and other RAF facilities from Japanese attacks and were given standard infantry training. They were also used to escort supply columns taking personnel, munitions and other supplies to RAF stations. Among the men coming ashore are a number of replacement Spitfire pilots, who needed to be taken to their air base. There was a critical shortage of landing ships and landing craft in Burma before late 1944, when some were released from the European theatre. (*Author's Collection*)

(**Opposite, below**) A British officer stops to admire a Japanese propaganda poster in the centre of Rangoon in May 1945. The poster shows an Imperial Army soldier stamping on the flags of the United Kingdom and the USA. This kind of propaganda had little effect on most Burmese, who were totally indifferent to both Allied and Japanese entreaties to support them. Most Burmese just wanted a quiet life and did not regard either side as liberators during the fighting. (*Author's Collection*)

Light 15cwt trucks cross a temporary wooden bridge near Pyu in the last stages of the advance on Rangoon. On the side of the truck's cab is stencilled the white five-pointed star which signified the Allied forces for most of the Second World War. The task of getting vehicles across the large number of rivers encountered during the Burma campaign was a constant problem. It required a great deal of both innovation and improvisation by the engineers of the Allied armies. (*Author's Collection*)

Immaculately turned-out soldiers of the 17th Indian Division are inspected by their commander, Major General 'Punch' Cowan. They wear the lucky Black Cat on a yellow patch on their shoulders, which replaced the previous lightning strike badge. The 17th had fought in Burma in 1942 and the Japanese propagandist Tokyo Rose disparagingly called the earlier badge the 'yellow streak'. It must have been gratifying for the troops of the 17th who had fought in 1942 that they helped liberate Rangoon, having been part of its garrison when it fell. (*Author's Collection*)

Chapter Fourteen

Japan's Defeat April–July 1945

After the fall of Meiktila and Mandalay in March 1945 and Rangoon in early May there were still sizeable formations of Japanese troops at large in southern and eastern Burma. The 14th Army's advance had bypassed large groups of Japanese, who would now have to be dealt with, while Japanese formations had regrouped in the country between Meiktila and the Yenangyuang oilfields to the west. There were also large groups of Japanese in the Karen Hills in eastern Burma, who were under increasing pressure from Kachin guerrilla forces. A large group of Japanese had redeployed to the east of the Rangoon-Toungoo road in the Sittang Valley. Another large formation of the 33rd Division was still operating to the north of Toungoo in the western Shan Hills. As well as the 14th Army's divisions the Japanese were also now under threat from the minority Burmese guerrillas. These were now under the control of the US Office of Strategic Services and were to prove a headache for the various Japanese enclaves. This was particularly the case in the hills of eastern Burma where Kachin, Karen, Chin and Shan tribes lived. Many of these tribesmen were out for revenge for Japanese atrocities against their populations from 1941 onwards. Any Japanese soldiers who fell into their hands could expect little mercy, and they received none. In addition, the ex-Burmese National Army units under the command of Aung San had joined the Allies on 28 March under the new title of the Patriot Burmese Forces. They were ready to attack their former allies as their leader attempted to achieve the independence the Japanese had offered him.

By May 1945 the remnants of the Japanese 28th Army had sought refuge in the Pegu Yomas mountain range between the Irrawaddy and Sittang rivers. General Sakurai's 30,000 men quickly set up a series of camps in the mountains, really a range of tall hills. The range ran for around 75 miles from north to south and 30 miles from west to east parallel to the Sittang river. Sakurai did not have much idea where any other formations of Japanese troops were as communications in the Imperial Army in Burma had virtually broken down. He was, however, aware that smaller groups of Japanese were waiting for the 28th Army to break out so that they could join them. There was a group of 2,000 troops who had congregated to the east of the Sittang river ready to cause a diversion to aid Sakurai's break-out. Other groups, survivors of the 15th and 33rd Armies who were not gathered in the Pegu Yomas, were on the west bank of the Sittang, also hoping to join with the 28th.

By late July it was obvious that the 28th Army could not sustain itself in the difficult terrain of the Pegu Yomas. Driven by the lack of food supplies, Sakurai decided to lead them out of the mountains to try to reach the safety of the Thai border. The men were formed into four large but manageable groups and were issued with their orders before leaving their mountain sanctuary. The escape route of the 28th would have to cross three rivers, the Yomas, the Sittang and the Salween. All his men were ordered to carry lengths of rope, and a 5m length of bamboo between two men. These would be used to build primitive rafts to get troops across the rivers, especially the wide Sittang. The planned day for the breakout was 20 July, but in reality it would take several days to get the large numbers of troops out of the mountains. As the 28th Army broke out of their mountain lairs, the 14th Army formations were waiting. On 4 August the better organised Japanese units were largely destroyed during a series of running battles with the 14th Army. The survivors of the initial break-out from the mountains headed for the main crossing point to the south of the British-held city of Toungoo. Heavy RAF attacks took place throughout the break-out, with a total of 3,000 sorties flown, dropping a total of 1,500,000lb of bombs and napalm on the fleeing troops, killing thousands of them. When large numbers of Japanese troops reached the Sittang river they fought desperately over the few large rafts and river boats available. Although some unit's crossings were well disciplined and organised, others were totally chaotic. In the absence of boats or rafts many attempted to swim across the fast-flowing river, but only the strongest had any chance of getting across safely. Most were too malnourished and weak to make the crossing, and several thousand were swept away in the fast-flowing currents. The exact number of dead is open to debate, although the 14th Army reported finding 11,500 bodies after the fighting. Out of the roughly 30,000 men of the 28th Army at the start of the break-out, there were a reported 13,593 men left at the end. In contrast, the 14th Army's casualties during the fighting against the 28th Army totalled only 435.

(**Opposite, above**) In this highly symbolic photograph Admiral Lord Louis Mountbatten sits on top of a captured 75mm Japanese field gun in Mandalay in April 1945 to make a speech to the tank crewmen who had manned the Shermans and other tanks that helped capture the city the day before. Lord Mountbatten had become Supreme Allied Commander of South-East Asia Command in late August 1943 and had proved to be an able and popular commander. Although he was a member of the royal family he had the knack of relating to the ordinary working-class men who made up the bulk of the British Army. (*Author's Collection*)

(**Opposite, below**) An honour guard of the Indian National Army's all-female Rani of Jhansi Regiment take part in a parade in early 1945. When the situation in Burma became too dangerous for the Indian Nationalist Subhas Chandra Bose, he decided to try to escape to Singapore. The young women of this regiment were allocated the job of guarding him on this long and arduous journey. They were attacked by Burmese bandits and several of the girls were killed in firefights or by Allied air attacks. (*Author's Collection*)

(**Above**) Shan guerrillas stand for inspection during a break in the fighting in eastern Burma in the early summer of 1945. The guerrillas are armed with a mixture of US Thompson sub-machine guns, Johnson automatic rifles and light machine guns and a Bren gun. Johnson rifles were developed for use with the US Marines but were considered too fragile for jungle use. They were used by the USA in some numbers, while others were handed out to the Allies and saw service with the Netherlands East Indies Army. Their uniforms appear to be a mixture of British woollen pullovers and US jungle green trousers and boots. (*US National Archives*)

(**Opposite, above**) Kachin commandos recruited and trained by the Office of Strategic Services pictured with their British trainer before going into action. The men are wearing jungle green uniforms in various shades, which were issued to them instead of the khaki drill uniforms. Two of the men have US M1 Garand rifles, while the other has a Bren gun over his shoulder. Their British comrade wears the same type of slouch hat as the Kachins, who all wear it with the left brim pinned up. (*Author's Collection*)

(**Opposite, below**) The Kachin commandos operating in the jungles of southern Burma were amongst the elite of the irregular forces in 1945. They were well trained to adapt their natural warrior traits to the modern jungle warfare they now faced. Arms were given out liberally to the Kachins, with the men pictured here having Thompson sub-machine guns and M2 carbines. Any Japanese who fell into their hands could expect little mercy following the brutal treatment of Burmese minorities from 1942 to 1945. (*US National Archives*)

The ground crew of a Mosquito FB ground-attack plane prepare their aircraft for a sortie in support of the 14th Army in early 1945. These aircraft spent the early months of the year destroying remaining Japanese strongholds, transport and other strategic targets. Their four 20mm Hispano cannon were devastating against soft targets and the Japanese had few places to hide as they withdrew through south-eastern Burma. (*Author's Collection*)

Left to right: Lieutenant Colonel Sir Montagu Stopford, commander of the 33rd Corps, Major General F.W. Messervy, commander of the 4th Corps, and Major General Douglas D. Gracey, commander of the 20th Indian Division, hold a roadside conference on the approaches to the city of Prome on 2 May 1945. The advance by the 33rd Corps between the Arakan Yomas and Pegu Yomas mountain ranges saw the capture of Prome on 3 May. (*Author's Collection*)

A signalman has climbed a telegraph pole to try to repair damage done by shelling in the recent fighting. The infrastructure of Burma had been badly affected by the bitter fighting, especially in cities and towns like Mandalay and Meiktila. Colonial Burma was never as well developed as in India in the pre-1941 era, and what infrastructure did exist was fragile. (*Author's Collection*)

Patriot Burmese Forces volunteers parade for their commander before going on a mission in the summer of 1945. Most of these anti-Japanese volunteers had previously served in the pro-Japanese Burmese National Army since 1942. Their leader Aung San negotiated with the Allies to 'turn traitor' against the Japanese and attack them. BNA personnel killed their military instructors and then took their revenge on any Japanese troops that fell into their hands. *(Author's Collection)*

British troops are transported in local boats to search for the remnants of the Japanese 28th Army after the break-out from the Pegu Yomas mountains. Tactics to trap the desperate Japanese included constant tank patrols and having large numbers of troops entrenched around strategic points. River crossing points and road junctions were guarded against units of Japanese who were trying to reach Thailand. *(Author's Collection)*

(**Above, left**) Soldiers land from civilian boats at village to the south of the town of Waw, 15 miles north-east of Pegu. Their orders were to root out any resistance from left-behind Japanese units. When intelligence was received that Japanese forces were still holding out, British and Indian forces would be despatched to winkle them out. Isolated Japanese troops often did not receive any orders apart from to resist and sell their lives dearly for the Emperor. The British and Indian troops had artillery and air support to call on if the Japanese proved stubborn. (*Author's Collection*)

(**Above, right**) A river boat full of British troops is steered across a river by a young Burmese who is willing to risk his life for the small payment he will receive. The rapid advance of the 14th Army through central Burma bypassed a large number of Japanese positions. Once the main objectives – Mandalay, Meiktila and Rangoon – had been taken, large numbers of British troops were sent out to hunt down and destroy any Japanese left behind. (*Author's Collection*)

A column of British soldiers march through the mud in pouring rain close to Pegu Canal, protected by their rain capes. It was a game of 'cat and mouse' between the retreating 28th Army who had come down from their Pegu Yomas hide-outs and their Allied pursuers. In July the Japanese had been driven by widespread hunger from the relative safety of the mountains. During the monsoon it usually rained torrentially for 10 hours per day, turning the Burmese countryside into a quagmire. The conditions meant that the British Army's armour and artillery in Burma were not always usable by the summer of 1945. (*Author's Collection*)

Two soldiers of the 1st Battalion, Queen's Royal Regiment, 7th Indian Division, stand down after the fighting for the Sittang Bend. The corporal wears the jungle green shirt with the black disc and red arrow badge of the 7th Division. Compared to his comrade, he is fairly well turned out, with a clean-looking slouch hat, which suggests he may be a recently arrived replacement. (*Author's Collection*)

(**Opposite, above left**) Returning from an operation against the 28th Army, Londoner Corporal R. Kemp washes the mud from his uniform. It was a miserable time for the British troops but at least when they returned to camp there were hot meals and dry tents to greet them. Their enemies were dying in their hundreds every day either in combat or from hunger and disease. Others drowned as they tried to cross rivers as they moved towards the final barrier of the Sittang river. (*Author's Collection*)

(**Opposite, above right**) Exhausted-looking British soldiers move through grasslands during the search for stay-behind Japanese troops. The Japanese fought a number of rearguard actions but some units withdrew in front of the 14th Army patrols. General Honda, the commander of the 33rd Division, left a note for the pursuing British in his abandoned headquarters; it read: 'General Honda was here, try harder next time.' (*Author's Collection*)

(**Opposite, below**) A pair of 5.5-in field guns fire towards a suspected Japanese position as the mopping-up of the Imperial Army's last holdouts in southern Burma continued. These guns are stationed on the approaches to Sittang, where some of the last of the organised Japanese formations were still fighting. The Japanese 33rd Division had counterattacked the 14th Army at the Sittang Bend but were beaten back by overwhelming firepower like this. (*Author's Collection*)

Pilots of the 607th Squadron, equipped with Spitfire Mk VIIIs, cross their sodden air strip after flying an attack on the Japanese along the west bank of the Sittang river. Two squadrons of Spitfires gave support to the British forces trying to block the retreat of the 28th Division. They operated along a 40-mile stretch of the Sittang where the main crossing points were located. During a nineteen-day period they destroyed seventy-five river craft and damaged 300 others, rendering them useless for the desperate Japanese. (*Author's Collection*)

A Valentine II Mk III bridge-laying tank. It carried a scissor bridge on the obsolete tank's chassis, which was tipped into position before it opened up with hydraulic arms and ramps. When unfolded, the bridge was 36ft long, which was sufficient to span most of the *chuangs* (streams) that would otherwise have delayed the Allied advance. Both the two Indian tank brigades and the 15th Corps in Arakan had a Royal Armoured Corps bridging troop attached to them. New equipment like the Valentine II enabled the rapid advance of the 14th Army's tanks and other vehicles. (*Author's Collection*)

In the rush to cut off the retreating 28th Division, a Sherman M4 medium tank crosses a small river on a scissor bridge, put in place by British Army engineers. Such bridges were portable and could be moved to another location when all the armoured vehicles had crossed. Burma's difficult terrain posed great challenges to both sides throughout the conflict, but by 1945 the Allies had the advantage of new equipment like this folding bridge to solve some of the problems. (*Author's Collection*)

Chapter Fifteen

The End of the Campaign

Although the fighting was coming to an end in southern Burma in August 1945, there were still groups of Japanese troops caught between the Sittang and Salween rivers. The main concentrations of Japanese still under arms were at the city of Moulmein on the far south and the towns of Kyaikto and Kyaukki. The various Japanese hold-outs were located and dealt with by the 14th Army, with most offered the opportunity to surrender. After years of hard fighting there was little patience with any Japanese who insisted on continued resistance, and they were dealt with ruthlessly. RAF air strikes on any Japanese units still under arms usually destroyed their will to continue to fight. The war in Asia was brought to an end when the atomic bombs were dropped on the Japanese cities of Hiroshima and Nagasaki on 6 and 9 August respectively. Emperor Hirohito's decision to accept defeat was made on the 10th and on the 15th he broadcast it to the Japanese nation. In Burma rumours had been circulating about the final defeat of Japan but not all Japanese commanders there were ready to accept the situation.

Japanese commanders in Burma were under the overall command of the Southern Area Army, with its headquarters at Saigon. The commander there, Field Marshal Terauchi, had had a cerebral haemorrhage when he heard of the fall of Mandalay in April 1945, but was left in post because his officers covered up his medical condition until the end of the war in August. On 10 August his headquarters received a report about the surrender of Japan, and on the 13th Terauchi called a conference of officers at which the prospect of further resistance was discussed. Plans had been in place for the substantial armies still under arms in South-East Asia to continue to fight the Allies, and Japanese armies on the Chinese mainland had similar plans to continue to resist, despite the official surrender. On 15 August Terauchi and his men listened to the broadcast by Emperor Hirohito, calling for the end of hostilities. On the 18th General Kimura signed the instruction commanding all Japanese troops to lay down their arms but it took until the 22nd for the first of a series of surrenders of the various Japanese formations. Some Japanese commanders refused to believe that their Emperor had agreed to surrender and were prepared to fight on. The 28th Army's commander, Sakurai, was still marching with his stragglers when he heard of the surrender. He and his men arrived at Moulmein and were officially informed by the commander there that the war was over.

On 28 August the surrender documents were signed in Rangoon by a group of Imperial Army, Navy and Air Force officers. General Slim found out about the Japanese surrender on 14 August but it was almost a month later when he joined Lord Louis Mountbatten to accept the Japanese surrender of all their forces in South-East Asia on 12 September. The cost of the Burma campaign had been heavy on both sides, with forces of the British Empire losing 70,000 killed. Japanese losses were listed as being 104,000 killed, although the true death toll may have been as high as 185,000. The rigours of jungle fighting had also left thousands of veterans suffering the effects of their service for many years, and in some cases for the rest of their lives.

The aftermath of the Burma campaign was to see a drastic change in the politics of the Indian subcontinent. India gained Independence from Britain in August 1947, and was divided into Hindu and Muslim states, India and Pakistan. This division was to cost millions of deaths in religious-based massacres which the British authorities were unable to control. An agreement was reached that would see Burma achieve genuine independence in 1948. The Burmese delegate to the talks was Aung San, the leader of the pro-Japanese Burmese National Army. The irony was that those who had sided with Japan in 1941–2 were favoured by the postwar agreements. Those who had served the Allies faithfully, like the Karen, Kachin and other minorities, were largely abandoned by their former allies. Aung San did not, however, live to enjoy the independence he had negotiated for his country. On 19 July 1947 he and many of his cabinet were assassinated by Sten gun-toting henchmen sent by his political rivals. Burma finally achieved independence on 4 January 1948 as the 'Union of Burma'.

Three broken and demoralised soldiers of the 28th Division wait to be processed after finally giving up the fight. They were among the 18,000 or so Japanese who had broken out of the Pegu Yomas mountains in July. When the survivors reached the Sittang river they tried to cross it even though it was swollen by monsoon water. Some crossed on improvised rafts while others swam across clinging to logs, trying to keep their mouths shut due to the danger of water leeches! (*Author's Collection*)

Japanese junior officers wade to a British post on the Sittang river to be interrogated by Allied intelligence officers. These men appear to be administrative personnel, as their smart uniforms indicate they haven't been in the front line. They were some of the fortunate 1,700 men taken prisoner; at least 10,000 of their comrades died trying to cross the Sittang. (*Cody Images*)

By the end of the Burma campaign many Japanese soldiers had been reduced to 'walking skeletons'. Imperial Army troops were reputed to be able to survive on a handful of rice a day, but this level of rations was not sustainable. These prisoners were captured after their attempts to cross the Sittang river had failed, and they were starving and exhausted. (*Author's Collection*)

(**Opposite, above**) Newly liberated British prisoners of war in Rangoon celebrate their freedom. They are holding the home-made flag they flew to show the advancing 14th Army troops where they were being held. When the Allied forces reached the Burmese capital, they found 1,000 prisoners, most of whom had been recently captured by the Japanese. (*Author's Collection*)

(**Opposite, below**) A group of British soldiers are safe at last after being abandoned by the retreating Japanese who took them prisoner in recent fighting. The emaciated condition of the soldiers is symptomatic of the harsh treatment meted out to captured Allied troops. The Japanese had enough problems feeding their own troops to bother about prisoners whom they regarded as expendable. These men were fortunate that their captors did not take the time to kill them and instead just left them to fend for themselves. (*Author's Collection*)

(**Above**) These Chindit prisoners of war, liberated by the British Army at the fall of Rangoon, look to be in fairly good health. They were captured during Operation Thursday in March 1944, so had not had to endure captivity for as long as some of their comrades. Soldiers who were captured in 1942 and 1943 were not in good condition after spending at least two years in Japanese hands. Thousands of Allied POWs died from neglect and cruelty, with starvation and many tropical diseases accounting for most. (*Author's Collection*)

Women drivers of the Auxiliary Territorial Service (ATS) arrive in Burma, having been shipped across the Bay of Bengal from Ceylon. The ATS was the women's branch of the British Army, and one of their main roles was driving ambulances and supply vehicles. On the home front the women, aged between 20 and 30, helped to man anti-aircraft guns and to keep communications open on all fronts. *(Author's Collection)*

A Japanese freight train moved into a siding by its crew is examined by British soldiers. It was one of the few trains that survived the constant bombing by the RAF and USAF during the Burma campaign. Once the Allies gained total air supremacy in 1944, little Japanese transport could safely move on the roads, rivers or railways. *(Author's Collection)*

Surrendered Japanese troops leave Rangoon on foot, pushing bicycles loaded with some of their belongings. They are watched by relaxed soldiers of the 5th Indian Division, who were relieved that the city fell without heavy casualties. Rangoon was abandoned by the Japanese in the first days of May when Allied reconnaissance aircraft flying over saw it was deserted. These Japanese handed themselves over to the authorities after the city had been taken over by the Allies. (*Cody Images*)

Japanese troops gather together on a railway as they prepare to surrender to the Allied forces in August 1945. Some Imperial Army soldiers were still full of fight when they were ordered to surrender but many others had simply had enough. Most of this group appear to be officers of various ranks, and their smart uniforms suggest they are from a rear unit. The officer with the *shin-gunto* sword will have to hand it over to the Allied authorities, even though it may be a family heirloom. (*Author's Collection*)

(**Above**) All over the Far East in late August 1945 groups of Japanese Imperial officers met with Allied officials to discuss surrender terms. This plane full of officers arrived at an airfield close to Rangoon to be met with Sten gun-wielding British troops. The swords that the officers wore when they arrived at these meetings were ceremonially surrendered to their Allied counterparts. Most of these *shin-gunto* swords had been passed down to the officers from their ancestors and the handing over of them was an extremely painful experience for them. (*Janusz Piekalkiewicz Collection*)

(**Opposite, above**) On Sunday, 26 August a number of high-ranking Japanese officers arrived at Ingahado airfield near Rangoon. In the left foreground of the group of officers is Lieutenant General Takazo Numata, who was chief of staff to Marshal Terauchi, the commander-in-chief of the Southern Army. The Japanese gave the Allies the information they needed in order to arrange the terms of surrender for Imperial Army formations in Burma. (*Author's Collection*)

(**Opposite, below**) The well turned-out pilots of the transport planes that brought the high-ranking Japanese officers are escorted away from their aircraft by British soldiers. The Japanese planes were painted white with red cross insignia on them to give them protection from Allied aircraft. It is ironic that the red cross was not usually recognised by the Japanese during the Burma campaign. (*Cody Images*)

In early September 1945 an immaculately turned-out officer of the Imperial Japanese naval landing troops surrenders to the Royal Navy at Rangoon naval base. Like all other Imperial armed forces officers, he is honour-bound to hand over his *shin-gunto* sword. Many of these swords were family heirlooms handed down from generation to generation, and it was regarded as a great loss of face by the officer to relinquish them to the enemy. (*Cody Images*)